MAPPING PROPERTY TAX REFORM IN SOUTHEAST ASIA

DECEMBER 2020

ASIAN DEVELOPMENT BANK

ADB

Notes:
In this publication, "$" refers to United States dollars.

On the cover: *Mapping Property Tax Reform in Southeast Asia* offers broader insight into the performance of recurrent
immovable property taxes. Property tax reforms in Cambodia, Philippines, Thailand, and Viet Nam can contribute to
broader government strategies and can benefit from coherence with other systems, as well as government functions
related to land management.

Cover design by Marjorie Ofaga

Contents

Tables and Figures

Foreword

Strengthening domestic resource mobilization through sound tax policies and administration is vital for developing member countries (DMCs) of the Asian Development Bank to meet the targets of the 2030 Agenda for Sustainable Development. The unprecedented coronavirus disease (COVID-19) crisis and the related containment measures have posed severe social and economic challenges to DMCs and may reverse years of progress on the development agenda. Based on the *Asian Development Outlook 2020 Update*, developing economies in Asia are expected to contract by 0.7% in 2020, making it the first regional recession in nearly six decades. Meeting the SDGs requires improvement in tax-to-GDP ratio in developing Asia. The effects of the economic downturn and the use of emergency tax relief measures during the COVID-19 pandemic will make that task more difficult and more urgent.

The road to recovery will need to address many issues including poverty, health, education, climate change, and promoting green and sustainable economic growth, with a renewed focus on tax issues to mobilize the resources needed. Improving tax compliance and international cooperation to prevent tax avoidance and evasion as well as broadening the tax base and exploiting underused revenue sources are all important.

This report on property tax reform is both timely and comprehensive. It provides an analysis of the property tax regime in Cambodia, the Philippines, Thailand, and Viet Nam in terms of the scope for increasing domestic resource mobilization, contributing to government strategies, maintaining coherence with other systems and government functions related to land management, and ensuring the robust design of the tax and the effectiveness of its administration.

Property taxes are underused in developing Asia, but they have significant revenue potential and could help governments narrow the inequality gap that has deepened with the impact of the COVID-19 crisis given its progressive nature. With this report, we in the Asian Development Bank sincerely hope to offer a broader insight into the performance of property taxes based on the experiences in Cambodia, the Philippines, Thailand, and Viet Nam. We are sure the report can also provide guidance for other DMCs engaging in property tax reform.

Woochong Um
Director General
concurrently Chief Compliance Officer
Sustainable Development and Climate Change Department
Asian Development Bank

Acknowledgments

The preparation of the report was led by Sissie Fung and Brian McAuley, consultants of the Asian Development Bank (ADB) Governance Thematic Group, Sustainable Development and Climate Change Department (SDCC). This benchmarking study is produced with financial support from the ADB Domestic Resource Mobilization Trust Fund (DRMTF) and the Japan Fund for Poverty Reduction (JFPR) with contribution from the Government of Japan. It presents a descriptive analysis of the recurrent property tax systems in four Southeast Asian countries: Cambodia, the Philippines, Thailand, and Viet Nam.

The authors wish to gratefully acknowledge the many people who contributed to this report, in particular the government officials from the following institutions with whom they consulted regularly: (i) from Cambodia—the Tax Policy Bureau and the Immovable Property Tax Bureau of the General Department of Taxation (Ministry of Economy and Finance) and the General Department Cadastre and Geography (Ministry of Land Management Urban Planning and Construction); (ii) from the Philippines—the Bureau of Local Government Finance (Department of Finance), the Land Registration Authority (Department of Justice), and the Land Management Bureau (Department of Environment and Natural Resources); (iii) from Thailand—the Fiscal Policy Office (Ministry of Finance), the Department of Lands (Ministry of Interior), and the Department of Local Administration (Ministry of Interior); and (iv) from Viet Nam—the Tax Policy Department and the General Department of Taxation (Ministry of Finance) and the General Department of Land Administration (Ministry of Natural Resources and Environment). This report would not have been completed without their valuable input and active participation in the in-country discussion meetings, the technical workshops, and final conference. The authors are especially grateful for the incredibly warm hospitality bestowed upon them during the data-gathering missions in the four countries.

The authors would like to thank the United Nations Economic and Social Commission for Asia and the Pacific (UN ESCAP) for co-organizing with ADB the technical workshop in Bangkok, Thailand, on 6 and 7 November 2018, at its headquarters and for providing invaluable support. The authors are also very grateful to all participants and ADB-invited speakers at the aforementioned workshop in Bangkok as well as at the technical workshop in Manila, the Philippines, in May 2019 and at the final property tax conference, also in Manila, in September 2019. With respect to the latter event, the authors would like to thank Naoyuki Yoshino, former dean of ADB Institute and our esteemed colleagues from ADB: Abdul Abiad, director of Macroeconomic Research Division; Hans van Rijn, principal public management specialist; and Seok Yong Yoon, principal public management specialist (e-Governance); as well as Justine Diokno-Sicat, research fellow from the Philippine Institute for Development Studies; and the international experts from UN ESCAP (Thailand), PASCO (Japan), VNG-International (Netherlands), and the French organizations IGNFI and CSN for their insightful contribution to the conference and sharing international best practices. Specifically, the authors would like to thank Zheng Jian, economic affairs officer of the Macroeconomic Policy and Financing for Development Division; UN ESCAP, and Stephane Gil, ADB consultant on land management, for their expert advice and collegial collaboration throughout this project, as well as Paul Carr, ADB consultant and international valuation reform implementation specialist, and Arjen Schep, endowed professor Taxes of Sub Central Governments at Erasmus School of Law, for their valuable comments on draft of this report. Finally, but certainly not the least, the authors would like to express their sincere gratitude to ADB colleagues from SDCC who facilitated the planning of in-country missions, workshops, and conference, in particular Christine Linaza. Special appreciation is also extended to Bruno Carrasco, Claudia Buentjen, Hanif Rahemtulla, Yasushi Suzuki, and Go Nagata for their ongoing support in this DRMTF benchmark study project and ADB's work on property tax reform.

The views expressed in this report are the authors' own and can in no way be taken to reflect the official opinion of ADB, ADB DRMTF, JFPR, or the Government of Japan. Notwithstanding the significant support provided from the above and many others, all mistakes made in this report are the authors' own.

Abbreviations

ADB	Asian Development Bank
BIR	Bureau of Internal Revenue (Philippines)
BLGF	Bureau of Local Government Finance (Philippines)
CAMA	computer-assisted mass appraisal
DENR	Department of Environment and Natural Resources (Philippines)
DMC	developing member country
DOL	Department of Lands
DRMTF	Domestic Resource Mobilization Trust Fund
eSRE	Electronic Statement of Receipts and Expenditures
GDP	gross domestic product
GDT	General Department of Taxation
GIS	geographic information system
IMF	International Monetary Fund
IRA	internal revenue allotment (Philippines)
LAO	local administrative organization (Thailand)
LGC	Local Government Code (Philippines)
LGU	local government unit (Philippines)
LIS	land information system
LMB	Land Management Bureau (Philippines)
MEF	Ministry of Economy and Finance
MLMUPC	Ministry of Land Management Urban Planning and Construction (Cambodia)
MOI	Ministry of Interior
MONRE	Ministry of Natural Resources and Environment (Viet Nam)
OECD	Organisation for Economic Co-operation and Development
PIN	Property Identification Number
PPC	Provincial People's Committee (Viet Nam)
RPT	Real Property Tax (Philippines)
SMV	schedule of market values (Philippines)
UCLG	United Cities and Local Governments
USAID	United States Agency for International Development

Currency Equivalents

(As of 31 December 2019)

Currency unit – riel (KHR)
KR1.00 = $0.0002457
$1.00 = KR4,070.00

Currency unit – peso (PHP)
₱1.00 = $0.01974
$1.00 = ₱50.6534

Currency unit –baht (THB)
B1.00 = $0.03360
$1.00 = B29.7600

Currency unit – dong (VND)
D1.00 = $0.0000431100
$1.00 = D23,196.47

Executive Summary

Background

As part of its Strategy 2030 with a vision for a prosperous, inclusive, resilient, and sustainable Asia and the Pacific, the Asian Development Bank (ADB) has confirmed its commitment to assist developing member countries (DMCs) to strengthen domestic revenue mobilization, enhance access to technology and innovation, and build capacity. Domestic public resources provide not only a more stable and sustainable source of income for developing countries to fund their development agenda; they also strengthen the social contract between the government and its citizens and foster good governance. As recognized by the Addis Tax Agenda, without effective mobilization of resources, the Sustainable Development Goals (SDGs) cannot be achieved. Property taxes are generally considered as "a good tax" for raising revenues in developing countries, especially in a time of globalization and increased international competition for mobile capital (Youngman 2016). ADB is committed to scale up its support to DMCs in their efforts to increase domestic revenue, including through fuller utilization of recurrent property taxes.

The objective of this study is to provide an analysis of the property tax regime in Cambodia, the Philippines, Thailand, and Viet Nam in terms of the scope for increasing domestic resource mobilization, the contribution to government strategies, the coherence with other systems and government functions related to land management, the design of the tax, and the effectiveness of the administration. This analysis can serve as a basis for DMCs to compare, evaluate, and improve the performance of property taxation and help foster broader policy discussions on reform opportunities. This report will also inform ADB's future operations on revenue mobilization and capacity development in the Asia and Pacific region.

Rationales for Property Taxation

Property taxation has significant revenue potential for developing countries and it is widely regarded as one of the best forms of taxation for promoting inclusive economic growth. Its merits include having a stable and expanding tax base with predictable revenue streams for governments, being economically efficient and relatively hard to evade due to asset immobility, and having the ability to contribute to social equity through redistributive policies that can help narrow the wealth gap. Property taxation is also increasingly seen as a policy tool to achieve other nonfiscal objectives, such as promoting efficient land use by increasing the costs of holding property vacant or underutilized, stabilizing house prices by curbing speculation in the real estate market, and capturing part of rising property values to finance urban infrastructure development and spur economic growth. As a local tax, property tax can play an important role in democratic local governance, and it has been argued that it allows the local population to hold their elected political leader accountable.

Yet despite its many favorable features and applications, governments in developing countries are only in recent years beginning to consider reforms to develop and maintain an efficient and effective property tax system. Their efforts are often complicated by additional, country-specific challenges, such as underdeveloped formal land markets, rapid urbanization, growth in informal settlements, diversity in land tenure and occupation, and large disparities in income and wealth. Attempts to improve the system have been difficult because of established special interests, political and institutional constraints, and shortcomings in the reform strategy of governments to address these challenges effectively. As pointed out in the literature, the main strategic shortcoming of reform efforts is either failure to clearly articulate the rationale for reform or having un-prioritized, contradictory objectives (Rosengard 2013).

Factors to Improve Revenue Performance: Key Findings

The four countries in this study all have some type of recurrent taxes on immovable property in place; some more than one. These property taxes, however, do not emerge as an important source of revenue, with reported revenue yield between 0.024% of gross domestic product (GDP) (Viet Nam) to 0.38% of GDP (Philippines) in 2017. Consistent with international practices, revenues from property taxes in the four countries are allocated to subnational government's budget, with varying degrees of local revenue autonomy. While property tax is one of the most important tax revenue sources for local governments, it represents only a small fraction of the overall subnational budget. Intergovernmental transfers and central government's grants and subsidies remain in most cases the mainstay of subnational income, which are often formula-based and not linked to the local tax mobilization efforts. This reliance on intergovernmental transfers and tax sharing may work as a disincentive for subnational governments to allocate resources to improving revenue raising from property taxation.

From the assessment of the main design features of property taxation (Chapter 4), property registration and fiscal cadastre (Chapter 5), and administrative arrangements (Chapter 6) in the four countries, the following factors can be addressed to improve revenue performance:

A. Policy Design Issues

- **Broaden the tax base.** All countries have a range of tax benefits in their tax code such as exemptions for government properties and historic and cultural sites, but also tax incentives for businesses operating in E-zones and tax reliefs to protect vulnerable taxpayers (e.g., by using basic property tax thresholds or exempting owner-occupied housing). These tax benefits significantly narrow the tax base and their objectives may be achieved in other ways.

- **Increase effective rates.** The statutory rates are generally low, with the effective rates even lower. Increases can be phased in over a number of years.

- **Use up-to-date market-price valuations.** Often assessed values do not reflect the current market value, either by design or due to constraints in administrative capacities. Regular revaluation of property is necessary to maintain buoyancy and to ensure fairness.

B. Cadastral Record-Keeping Issues

- **Modernize data infrastructure.** Among the principal prerequisites for effective property taxation are adequate systems of property registration and fiscal cadastre that contain complete and up-to-date information about ownership, rights, actual use, sales prices, parcel boundaries, and other characteristics of immovable properties. Such systems can produce statistical data to support evidence-based revenue forecasting and decision-making on property tax reform, provide better estimates of the market value of properties, and improve the efficiency and effectiveness in administering and collecting property taxes. In most countries, the functions and responsibilities for the maintenance of the land registry and fiscal cadastre, as well as the titling, valuation, surveying, and mapping of properties, are carried out by different tiers of government and organizations under different ministries, resulting in fragmented data keeping.

- **Cooperation in government data sharing.** A common concern raised among the countries is the lack of coordination between government organizations on the systematic exchange of records and/or the lack of data compatibility between the different information systems. Ensuring a smooth data flow, as well as safeguarding accountability of the different government institutions involved, are essential for the effective administration of the property tax.

- **Secure reliable data on recent sales prices.** Market value assessment is based on comparable sales prices between a willing buyer and a willing seller in an arm's length transaction. In some instances, reliable data on recent sales and listing prices are not readily available due to the absence of developed property markets. As markets develop especially in urban areas, action is needed to capture actual data and counter the underreporting of transactions to evade property transfer taxes.

C. Administrative Issues

- **Strengthen financial and human resources.** Effective implementation of property taxation requires adequate administrative capacity (i.e., sufficient financial and human resources). A common issue in developing countries is the scarcity of qualified property assessors. New technologies, such as computer-assisted mass appraisal (CAMA) system with geographic information system (GIS), satellite-aided mapping, and cross-referencing data between intergovernmental agencies, can lower the ongoing administrative costs and change the way governments are administering their property taxes. However, implementing such technologies would require a significant upfront investment.

- **Improve taxpayer compliance.** Most countries in this study rely on a system of self-assessment, where taxpayers are required to register, declare, value, and/or calculate the assessments on their properties. Self-assessment can be an appealing procedure, particularly in countries with limited administrative capacity, as it is relatively easy to implement while keeping the administrative costs for governments low. However, such systems will inherently result in undertaxation, unless significant penalties are put in place and effectively enforced to deter nonreporting and underreporting.

- **Implement standards for valuation practices.** Valuation is a major administrative challenge in virtually all developing countries. Setting and monitoring common standards will protect revenues and avoid regional disparities in property valuation.

Benchmarking Reform Strategies

Property tax reform generally serves one or more of the following objectives (Rosengard 2013, with reference to Muellbauer 2005):

1. Raising revenue for government to fund public goods and services;

2. Improving social equity by assuring a fair tax burden distribution among taxpayers;

3. Enhancing economic efficiency by minimizing the distortional impact of the property tax on economic behavior; and

4. Improving the administrative cost-effectiveness of the tax system through simplification, standardization, and automation.

The four countries in this study have each adopted different strategies and are at varying stages of reform, but they all share the common principal objective of improving the revenue performance of the property tax regime. Both Viet Nam and Thailand have undertaken a comprehensive approach to overhaul the property tax system by replacing and merging the existing taxes and moving toward a modern property tax. While Viet Nam is still carrying out a comprehensive property tax reform study, Thailand's Land and Building Tax came into effect on 1 January 2020. With, among others, a broader tax base, higher rates for vacant land, and a movement away from a rental value to a market value approach, the new tax is expected to yield B40 billion after a phase-in period of 3 years: an increase of 17% in tax revenue. Cambodia has taken a more cautious approach to enhancing the revenue performance of the immovable property tax by focusing on administrative improvements that expand the tax base coverage, increase the valuation level, and strengthen the enforcement and compliance measures, while conducting further studies to improve social equity and raising more revenue. The Philippines has the most decentralized property tax system of the jurisdictions targeted in this study; however, local disparities in property valuation have affected the revenue performance of the real property tax (RPT). Philippines' Real Property Valuation and Assessment Reform Act (House Bill No. 4664) aims to improve the quality and uniformity of the real property valuation system by adopting internationally accepted valuation standards, concepts, principles, and practices, and recentralizing the approval of the schedule of market values by local government units back to the secretary of Finance. At the time of writing of this report, the bill has advanced to the final stages of the legislative process. In Chapter 3 of this report, Table 3 provides an overview of the reform strategies in the four countries.

Recommendations on the Way Forward

With the recent reform initiatives, the four countries have taken a positive step toward sustained revenue mobilization. In the medium and long terms, substantial additional revenues are possible, but a strategy for such increases must be carefully designed to the individual country's particular circumstances and applied gradually to avoid sudden impacts, particularly on vulnerable taxpayers, and compensating measures may be required for them. Increasing the property tax revenue to 1% (or more) of GDP would deliver significant benefits to the country and setting such a goal for, say, 5 to 10 years hence could establish a context for the continuous improvement of the system and administration of property tax.

This report concentrates on the revenue raising goals of property taxation and recognizes that other government strategies may be supported by the design of property taxation. It is noted that property tax can be a policy instrument to promote efficient land use management, for example, by increased tax rates for unused property, which may also be supportive of infrastructure development. It is generally accepted that a well-designed property tax based on market valuations can have an effect on stabilization of residential property prices and can play a role in land value capture. The relationship with fiscal decentralization is more nuanced: while there is scope for property tax to make a bigger contribution to local government finance, fiscal decentralization has not been a driver of resource mobilization in low-income developing countries. These issues merit further attention and in particular the issue of land value capture is increasingly relevant for developing countries in the region experiencing accelerated development in urban areas.

The relationship between property taxation and land management brings into play the opportunities that e-government approaches to data and technology can provide. We note and welcome the current studies within ADB to support the coordinated development of comprehensive land management information systems that can provide a sound basis for a fiscal cadastre and be deployed for a range of purposes encompassing land and resource management and social and environmental protection.

I. Introduction

As part of its Strategy 2030 with a vision for a prosperous, inclusive, resilient, and sustainable Asia and the Pacific,[1] the Asian Development Bank (ADB) has confirmed its commitment to assist developing member countries (DMCs) to strengthen domestic revenue mobilization, enhance access to technology and innovation, and build capacity. Domestic public resources provide not only a more sustainable source of income for developing countries to fund their development agenda; they also strengthen the social contract between the government and its citizens and foster good governance. As recognized by the Addis Tax Agenda, without effective mobilization of resources, the Sustainable Development Goals cannot be achieved. Property taxes are generally considered as a "good tax" for raising revenues in developing countries, especially in a time of globalization and increased international competition for mobile capital (Youngman 2016).

Why Property Taxation?

Property taxation is regarded to be among the best forms of taxation for contributing to social equity and economic efficiency; while providing a stable and predictable revenue source for governments (Norregaard 2013). According to Rosengard, property taxation is adopted because it is

- Relatively difficult to evade, due to the high visibility and immobility of property;
- Economically efficient and easy to enforce though seizure and liquidation of property;
- Significant in terms of its revenue-raising capacity;
- A relatively stable and predictable revenue source, as well as adjustable through incremental rate changes;
- Generally progressive for residential property because the tax burden is predominantly borne by middle- and high-income earners; and
- Less distortive than other tax instruments in terms of its effects on long-term economic growth and the least affected by globalization (Rosengard 1998).[2]

In addition, as a revenue source for subnational governments, property taxation may also enhance local autonomy through the elicitation of greater government responsiveness and accountability (Rosengard 1998).

---

[1]   ADB. 2018. *Strategy 2030: Achieving a Prosperous, Inclusive, Resilient, and Sustainable Asia and the Pacific.* Manila.
[2]   According to the Organisation for Economic Co-operation and Development (OECD), recurrent taxes on immovable property are the least distortive instrument in terms of reducing long-run gross domestic product (GDP) per capita, followed by consumption taxes and other property taxes, environmentally related taxes, personal income taxes, and corporate income taxes. OECD. 2010. Tax Policy Reform and Economic Growth. *OECD Tax Policy Studies.* Paris. See also Brys et al. 2016. Tax Design for Inclusive Economic Growth. *OECD Taxation Working Papers.* No. 26. Paris: OECD.

Although most countries have some sort of system of taxing land and/or buildings, the revenue performance of property taxes remains low in developing countries. Attempts to improve the system have been difficult because of established special interests, political and institutional constraints, and shortcomings in the reform strategy of governments to address these challenges effectively. As pointed out in the literature, the main strategic shortcoming of reform efforts is either failure to articulate clearly the rationale for reform or having unprioritized, contradictory objectives (Rosengard 2013).

Against this background, this chapter attempts to offer broader insight into the rationale and strategic goals of property taxes.

Rationales for Property Taxation

Taxation on land and property has both fiscal and nonfiscal effects. Apart from its prime purpose in raising revenue for governments, property taxes can be an important instrument to capture land value, promote efficient land use management and infrastructure development, and stabilize residential property prices. It has also been seen as a tool to support fiscal decentralization.

Raising Domestic Revenue to Meet the Sustainable Development Goals

Mobilizing domestic revenue is a key issue on the international financing for development agenda. Domestic public resources are a more stable and sustainable source of income; they also strengthen a legitimate relationship between citizens and the state and foster good governance.[3] As set out in the Addis Ababa Accord, "the mobilization and effective use of domestic resources, underscored by the principle of national ownership, are central to our common pursuit of sustainable development, including achieving the Sustainable Development Goals."[4]

Property tax has great revenue potential and represents one of the largest sources of untapped revenue for developing countries (Norregaard 2013). Whereas in high-performing countries like France and the United Kingdom property tax revenues could reach up well over 4% of the gross domestic product (GDP),[5] in many Asian developing countries, such as the Philippines, Thailand, and Indonesia, property tax revenue yielded between 0.1% and 0.5% of GDP in 2017.[6] The yield by other DMCs in the region is even lower. Experience suggests that even modest investments in reform to land and property tax systems can help countries dramatically expand tax revenues to finance their own development and reduce their dependency on foreign aid (Collier et al. 2017). Another positive feature of property taxation is the relative stability of its tax base. As the value of land and properties are rising in virtually all countries due to population growth and land developments—and subsequently widening the gap between the haves and have-nots—property taxes constitute a stable and an expanding tax base.

Capturing Land Value

Asia urbanizes at an unprecedented rate. As the urban population is growing, so is the public demand for sustainable infrastructure development, such as quality mass transit systems, affordable housing, community amenities, and other public service provision. However, local governments in many developing cities are constrained by limited

---

[3]   The Addis Tax Initiative–Declaration. https://www.addistaxinitiative.net/sites/default/files/resources/ATI-Declaration-EN.pdf.
[4]   United Nations. 2015. *Addis Ababa Action Agenda of the Third International Conference on Financing for Development.* New York. para. 20.
[5]   OECD. 2018. *Revenue Statistics 2018.* Paris. This includes not only "recurrent" property taxes, but also taxes on property transfers and other property-based taxes, such as wealth tax and inheritance tax.
[6]   OECD. 2019. *Revenue Statistics in Asian and Pacific Economies.* Paris.

resources to carry out the necessary public investment. At the same time, prices of land and properties is increasing due to urban population growth, which places higher demand on land. As all public investment in goods and services feeds into urban land values, there is a strong argument for governments to capture some of these increases in land and property prices that are the result of external effects, such as natural population increase, rural–urban migration, speculation, and reclassification of rural land to urban land. Property owners, in particular those that are passive beneficiaries in terms of rising property values due to these external factors, are becoming effortlessly richer (the so-called "getting richer while sleeping" effect) (Salm 2017).

Land value capture is an approach to finance urban infrastructure development and ensures that governments can capitalize on the economic windfall gains from investments and subsequently reinvest the revenues in public goods and services to create more value, enabling a virtuous cycle and an engine for sustained economic growth. One of the mechanisms to capture land value is though the taxation system, either through the mainstream taxes, such as income, sales, and property taxes, or through special levies and charges enacted for one-off purposes. An example of the latter, which targets a specifically defined beneficiary base, is the betterment levy. Typically, this is levied on beneficiaries of an infrastructure investment (such as a major transit upgrade) who see a significant increase of their property value due to the economic impact of the upgrade. The betterment levy is outside the scope of this report and is not in evidence in the countries covered. However, the Philippine government is currently considering introducing a national betterment levy with the establishment of an infrastructure fund that aims to capture increased value of properties that have benefited by government projects, such as the Build, Build, Build Program.[7] Other examples of special fees and levies relating to transit investments include connection fees and rezoning fees (Abiad et al. 2019).

Property tax is generally considered to be the tax with the highest potential to partially capture the value created by new infrastructure investments through the increase of property value in the tax base and the corresponding tax liability (Cornia 2013).

Promoting Efficient Land Use

Property taxes can be utilized as a policy instrument to influence land use patterns by adding costs or providing incentives to develop land or leave it undeveloped. In general, property taxes increase the costs of holding land or keeping property vacant and underutilized; they therefore provide incentives to land and property owners to recover the tax costs and put their immobile asset to its most valuable use. Property development becomes more attractive, in particularly in areas where land values are high (Muellbauer 2005, Blöchliger 2015). Property tax can thus promote efficient land use, particularly if market price valuation or higher rate for unused land is applied, thereby stimulating development and growth. There is an economic case for a pure land tax in the literature, as opposed to the conventional property tax on land and buildings; it has been argued that the inclusion of buildings in the tax base would reduce the incentive to improve land because of the corresponding increase in tax burden, whereas a pure land tax would be neutral in its impact on land development decisions (Brandt 2014). However, countries with pure land taxes are rare, so there is little empirical evidence available to draw any firm conclusions (Brandt 2014). In addition, considering the narrow tax base, land taxes would require much higher tax rates in order to yield the same revenue as a traditional property tax, which might encounter political resistance. Furthermore, as the selling price of properties generally does not make a distinction between land price and building price, establishing the current market value of land alone may add another layer of complexity to the valuation and administration of the tax. Viet Nam, for example, which currently taxes land only, is moving toward a land and building tax to generate more revenues from its property tax regime while curbing speculation in the residential real estate market.

[7]   P.P. Quizon. 2019. *The Philippines Valuation Reform*. Presentation prepared for the ADB Conference on Property Tax Reform and Domestic Resource Mobilization in Asia and the Pacific Region. Manila. 16–18 September.

Most countries have incentivizing policies in their property tax regime to achieve certain land use goals, such as low rates or exemptions for farmland and forests to prevent conversion to urban development. More recently, some countries have sought to use property tax as an environmental policy instrument to promote investments in energy efficiency or renewable energy through property tax rebates (Brandt 2014). The state of Indiana (in the United States), for example, offers a tax deduction to property owners who have installed eligible renewable energy systems such as solar, wind, and geothermal technologies.[8] The overall opinion on the effectiveness of such schemes is largely skeptical, since tax expenditures are costly, may create unwanted side effects, or even fail to reach their stated objective (Brandt 2014, Blöchliger 2015).

Stabilizing House Prices

Rapid urbanization has driven up residential property prices dramatically. Property taxes can be used as a policy instrument to dampen the volatility and rapid rise of house prices. An Organisation for Economic Co-operation and Development (OECD) study suggests that increasing property tax revenues that evolve in line with rising property prices—through regular updates of property values—can act as an automatic (countercyclical) stabilizer on the housing market (OECD 2016). Empirical analysis from the OECD shows that increasing the property-tax-to-GDP ratio from 0.5% to 1% would curb house price volatility between 1% and 4%, while slowing the growth of house prices. Conversely, countries with low property taxation and less frequent property revaluations tend to show steeper house price fluctuation, although the effect is rather small (Blöchliger 2015).

To curb speculation in the real estate market, the People's Republic of China, for example, is on the verge of introducing a property tax with the objective to curb speculation and rising housing prices (Salm 2017). High taxes on immovable properties can have the benefit of shifting investment out of speculative housing into more productive, higher-return activities and so increase the rate of growth.

Promote Fiscal Decentralization and State Building

For a variety of reasons, some developing countries have embarked on fiscal decentralization programs, which increase the ability of subnational government to raise finances for local service delivery and development. There are many virtues ascribed to decentralization: it is claimed to produce more efficient and equitable local service delivery, enhance democracy, encourage participation in local development activities, and thus result in more popular support for government and in improved local political stability and accountability (Bird and Vaillancourt 1998). However, these results are observed more in developed countries than in developing ones.

There are generally three major sources for financing local governments: intergovernmental transfers, subnational taxes, and other revenues (e.g., service charges, registration fees, licenses, permits, and royalties). Strengthening the subnational tax system can help reduce the reliance of local governments on intergovernmental transfers, thereby improving economic efficiency through enhanced local accountability. According to Bird and Vaillancourt, subnational taxes should ideally be sufficient enough for subnational governments to finance all their services to local residents, and be collected from local residents only, preferably in relation to the perceived benefits they receive from local services (Bird and Vaillancourt 1998). To this end, subnational taxes should have the following characteristics:

- The tax base should be relatively immobile.
- The revenue yield should be adequate to meet local needs and sufficiently buoyant over time.

---

[8]   Indiana Office of Energy Development: https://www.in.gov/oed/2379.htm.

- The revenue yield should be relatively stable and predictable over time.

- It should have no or limited possibility for tax exporting to nonresidents.

- The tax base should be visible to ensure transparency and accountability.

- The tax should be perceived as fair by taxpayers.

- The tax should be relatively easy to administer (Bird and Vaillancourt 1998).

Property tax is widely considered to be the appropriate tax to provide local governments meaningful revenue autonomy in fiscally decentralized systems. Besides having an immobile tax base and a relatively stable tax yield, property tax is a good local tax because its tax burden is largely borne by local residents who benefit from local public services and goods such as schools, libraries, roads, transit, water and electricity infrastructure, garbage collection, and neighborhood parks. It can thus be seen as a charge for local government services (the "benefit view"), and therefore not only as an efficient tax but also as a fair tax (Bahl and Martinez-Vazquez 2007). It is asserted that when property taxes finance local services, public sector decisions will tend to be more responsive to taxpayers' needs (Slack and Bird 2014). It has also been argued that local authorities would be more fiscally responsible, that is, less likely to overspend based on the expectation that tax exporting would allow them to pass some of the tax burden to nonresidents (Bahl and Martinez-Vazquez 2008). Property tax plays a key role in the democratic local governance process because it allows the local population to hold their elected political leader accountable. It is a highly visible and thus a transparent tax: those liable know the amount they pay each year and can use this information to hold their elected officials accountable for services delivered (Bahl 2009).

As observed by Bird and Slack (2002), this view inherently assumes that (i) property taxes in fact finance public services that benefit property values, (ii) the tax rates and service levels are decided by local voters, (iii) taxpayers who want other combinations of services and tax rates can freely move to other jurisdictions, (iv) voters—impelled by their sensitivity to property values—act rationally in response to such signals, and (v) local governments are responsive to needs of their constituents. The strength and validity of many of these assumptions, however, might be ambiguous in many countries. Of course, the level of local autonomy, either desired or actually attained, varies greatly among countries and much depends on the historical and institutional discourse of the intergovernmental relations within the country, its internal politics, administrative capacity, technical and political constraints, and so on. Where financing is from property tax and from fiscal transfers, local politicians have sometimes sought to maximize fiscal transfers in order to limit the revenue raised from local taxes, thus undermining the potential for domestic resource mobilization.

Despite the promise of improved public service delivery, greater inclusiveness, and enhanced local accountability, fiscal decentralization in the developing world has produced mixed results. In some cases, the efficiency and effectiveness of local service delivery has, in fact, decreased due to weak local government capacity in, for example, planning, accounting, and budget implementation as well as poor civil service management. Fiscal decentralization has also brought challenges of its own. It has sometimes sacrificed economies of scale and central government control over scarce domestic resources, produced greater regional disparities and fiscal imbalances, and made policy coordination among levels of government more difficult (Usui 2007). National and local governments have also clashed over what should be done even though each is aiming to serve its constituents. Furthermore, local decision-making processes can also be captured by the local elite (Usui 2007).

Scope and Methodology

This report analyzes the recurrent property tax systems in four Southeast Asian countries: Cambodia, the Philippines, Thailand, and Viet Nam. The four countries are at different stages of reform and were part of ADB's Domestic Resource Mobilization Trust Fund (DRMTF) benchmarking study on property tax reform. The benchmark exercise was a 12-month project, designed to enhance opportunities for collaboration and knowledge sharing between participating DMCs and focused on the following pillars of property taxation: (i) the policy rationale, (ii) the design features (tax base, tax rate, valuation), (iii) fiscal cadastre and land management, and (iv) the administrative arrangements. Within each pillar, a questionnaire was developed to gather information from the four countries, followed up with in-country missions to conduct interviews with government officials from the Ministry of Finance, General Department of Taxation, Ministry of Land Management and Natural Resources and/or Ministry of Interior. Each pillar was concluded with a draft report and subsequently discussed among the four countries in two closed workshops.

This final report is a consolidation of the draft reports, input resulting from the questionnaires, interviews, email exchanges, workshops, and additional research. A draft version of this report was presented at the final conference in Manila, Philippines, on 16–18 September 2019.

Table 1:   Workshops and Conference

Date	Event	Location	People Interviewed and/or Attending
6–7 November 2018	Workshop on rationale and strategic goals of property taxes and on policy elements (tax base, tax rate, and valuation) of property taxes (pillars 1 and 2)	Bangkok, Thailand (held at UN ESCAP)	Government officials of Cambodia, Thailand, and the Philippines with responsibility for tax policy and property tax administration, as well as international experts.
9–10 May 2019	Workshop on property registration and fiscal cadastre (pillar 3)	Manila, Philippines (ADB headquarters)	Government officials of Cambodia, the Philippines, Thailand, and Viet Nam with responsibility for tax policy, property tax administration and land management, as well as international experts.
16–18 September 2019	Conference on property tax reform and domestic resource mobilization in the Asia and Pacific region	Manila, Philippines (Crowne Plaza Hotel)	Government officials of Cambodia, the People's Republic of China, Indonesia, Lao People's Democratic Republic, Malaysia, Mongolia, the Philippines, Thailand, and Viet Nam with responsibility for tax policy, property tax administration and land management, as well as international experts and development partner (UN ESCAP).

ADB= Asian Development Bank, UN ESCAP = United Nations Economic and Social Commission for Asia and the Pacific.
Source: Authors.

The Organization of the Report

This report has seven chapters. The next chapter "Taxing Property in Asia" provides an overview of the different types and classification of property taxes in the four benchmarking countries. The third chapter "Property Tax Reform: Rationales and Benchmark of Strategies", describes the primary rationales for initiating property tax reform, the current issues regarding the property tax system, and subsequently, the reform strategies deployed or under consideration in the four countries to address those issues. Chapter 4 "Main Design Features of Property Taxation" gives a descriptive analysis of the policy elements of the property tax regime: the tax subject, tax base, tax rate, valuation, and tax exemptions and reliefs. The fifth chapter presents information on the property registration system and fiscal cadastre, and Chapter 6 details the administrative arrangements (e.g., tax assessment; billing, collection, and enforcement; and tax appeal). The final chapter discusses the conclusion of this study and recommendations on the way forward.

II.   Taxing Properties in Asia

What are property taxes? This chapter provides an overview of the different types and classification of property taxes in the four benchmarking countries, the revenue share in terms of tax-to-GDP ratio, and the overall reliance on the property tax as local income source for subnational governments.

Types of Taxes on Property

Taxes on property are generally understood to cover all types of recurrent and nonrecurrent taxes and levies on the use, ownership, and transfer of property. These include (i) recurrent taxes on immovable property; (ii) recurrent taxes on net wealth; (iii) taxes on estates, inheritances, and gifts; (iv) taxes on financial and capital transactions (e.g., stamp duties, registry fees, and property transfer taxes); and (v) other nonrecurrent and recurrent taxes on property (e.g., betterment levies to capture land value increases). Taxes on rental income and capital gain derived from real property are considered taxes on income (personal or corporate), and thus not classified as taxes on property for the purpose of this study. This categorization of taxes on property largely follows the International Monetary Fund (IMF), OECD, and the European Union's definition and schemes for classifying taxes in their respective tax revenue statistics, although some variations exist.[9]

Overview of Taxes on Property in Southeast Asia

The four benchmarking countries all have different types of taxes on property. As illustrated in Table 2, some countries have more than one recurrent tax on immovable property, but none of the countries have recurrent taxes on net wealth (i.e., taxes on a wide range of movable and immovable property, net of debt, paid by either individuals or corporate enterprises). Some countries have special local levies on immovable properties to provide additional income sources to local government units (LGUs). In the Philippines, for example, a Special Levy may be imposed on lands that have benefited by public work projects financed by the local government. The local authorities in the Philippines may also impose other additional levies on real properties, whose revenue is earmarked for specific purposes, such as the Special Education Fund Tax for public education and the Socialized Housing Tax for low-income housing projects. These levies are categorized under other nonrecurrent and recurrent taxes on property.

A Creditable Withholding Tax is levied by the Philippines on real estate transactions on the sale, transfer, or exchange of real property classified as ordinary asset. As this tax is creditable against the income tax payable of

---

9   IMF. 2014. *Governance Finance Statistics Manual 2014.* Washington, DC: International Monetary Fund; *OECD, 2018. Revenue Statistics 1965–2017, Interpretative Guide.* Paris: OECD Publishing; EU. 2019. *Taxation Trends in the European Union, Data for the EU Member States, Iceland and Norway.* Luxembourg: Publication Office of the European Union.

the seller and thus acts as an advanced payment of the seller's income tax, the Creditable Withholding Tax is classified as "Taxes on income, profits, and capital gains" and not considered as a tax on property, for the purpose of this study.

Effective since 1 February 2016, Thailand has introduced an inheritance tax and a gift tax. The latter is in reality a tax on income, profits, and capital gains, as gifts of immovable property are subjected to personal income tax. Thailand also has a Specific Business Tax, which applies a 3% rate to the gross proceeds from the sale of immovable property or real estate in a commercial or profitable manner. In addition, a municipal tax of 10% is applied. The Specific Business Tax is imposed on certain businesses that are excluded from Value-Added Tax and can be classified as "Taxes on goods and services."

In Viet Nam, the property transfer tax (the Law on Land Use Transfer Tax), which applied a tax rate of 2% or 4% to the transfer of land use rights depending on the type of land, was replaced by the corporate and personal income tax in 2004. Capital gain derived from a transfer of land use right is currently subject to 20% income tax. In the event that the purchase price and the expenses related to the real estate transfer cannot be determined, an income tax equal to 2% of the transfer price must be paid. These taxes are classified as "Taxes on income, profits, and capital gains."

Table 2 provides an overview of the different types of taxes on property in the four countries.

Table 2:   Taxes on Property

Country	Name of Instrument	Levied at National or Sub-national Level	Recurrent Immovable Property	Inheritance and Gift	Financial and Capital Transfer	Other
Cambodia	Tax on Immovable Property	National (earmarked for local budget)	✓			
	Tax on Unused Land	National (earmarked for local budget)	✓			
	Registration Tax (transfer Tax)	National (earmarked for local budget)			✓	
Philippines	Real Property Tax	Subnational	✓			
	Idle Land Tax	Subnational	✓			
	Estate Tax (inheritance tax)	National		✓		
	Donor's Tax (gift tax)	National		✓		
	Transfer Tax	Subnational			✓	
	Special Education Fund Tax	Subnational				✓
	Special Levy	Subnational				✓
	Socialized Housing Tax	Subnational				✓
	Documentary Stamp Tax	National			✓	

Table 2:   Taxes on Property (*continued*)

| Country | Name of Instrument | Levied at National or Sub-national Level | Taxes on Property | | | |
			Recurrent Immovable Property	Inheritance and Gift	Financial and Capital Transfer	Other
Thailand	Land and Building Tax	Subnational	✓			
	Inheritance Tax	National		✓		
	Property Transfer Fee	Subnational			✓	
	Stamp Duty Tax	National			✓	
Viet Nam	Non-Agricultural Land Use Tax	National (earmarked for local budget)	✓			
	Agricultural Land Use Tax	National (earmarked for local budget)	✓			
	Registration Fee	National (earmarked for local budget)			✓	

Source: Authors' data based on the data gathered from the General Department of Taxation (GDT) of Cambodia, the Bureau of Local Government Finance (BLGF) of the Philippines, the Fiscal Policy Office (FPO) of Thailand, and the Ministry of Finance of Viet Nam.

Cambodia

Tax on Immovable Property. The Tax on Immovable Property was introduced under the 2010 Law on Financial Management and became effective in 2011. Under this law, a 0.1% recurrent tax is applied on immovable properties located in a limited number of urban areas. The tax base is 80% of the assessed market value of the property minus a general exemption of KHR100 million (approx. USD 25,000). The market value is assessed and updated on a regular basis by the Immovable Properties Appraisal and Valuation Commission, under the political responsibility of the minister of Economy and Finance. Certain immovable properties are exempted, such as agricultural land; properties belonging to the government, religious or charitable institutions, diplomatic or consular mission, and international organizations; public infrastructure; immovable properties located in special economic zones; and houses, buildings, and structures that are under construction (less than 80% completed) and have not yet been used (Fung and McAuley 2020). Like most property taxes, the Tax on Immovable Property is a local government tax, whose revenue is allocated to the subnational government (cities, provinces, towns, districts, *khans,* communes, and *sangkats*) for its regional development. *Khans* are part of the middle tier of local government comprising districts, municipalities, and *khans.* They are only located within the capital, Phnom Penh. A *sangkat* or commune is the lowest tier of local government in the country. Communes are located within the rural districts, and *sangkats* are located within provincial municipalities or the capital.

Tax on unused land. Introduced in 1995, the Tax on Unused Land is levied on unused land, including unused land with existing buildings in an abandoned state, at a rate of 2% tax of the assessed market value of the land per square meter (Fung and McAuley 2020).

Property transfer tax. A 4% registration tax is levied on the transfer value or the assessed market value as determined by the Immovable Property Assessment Committee (whichever is higher) for the transfer of ownership or right of possession of immovable property. Transfer among relatives, however, is exempted for registration tax, but might be subjected to preferential duties (Fung and McAuley 2020).

Philippines

Real property tax. The Real Property Tax (RPT) is an annual recurrent ad valorem tax on real properties, with ceiling rates set at 1% for properties located in a province and 2% for properties located in a city or a municipality within the Metropolitan Manila Area. The tax is based on the assessed value, which is calculated by applying the assessment levels to the market value of the property. The LGUs have discretionary powers to set the rates and assessment levels. The RPT is a local-level tax, imposed and administered by LGUs under the Local Government Code (LGC) of 1991.

Idle land tax. The Idle Land Tax is an (optional) additional levy on the assessed value of lands that are classified as idle at a ceiling rate of 5% per annum (Sections 236–239 of the LGC 1991).

Estate tax. Estate Tax is levied on the value of the net estate of a descendent, determined as of the time of death, at a rate of 6%.[10] Real properties are valued at the higher of the fair market value as determined by the commissioner of the Bureau of Internal Revenue (BIR), and the fair market value as determined in the schedule of values fixed by the provincial and city assessors (Section 88 of the National Internal Revenue Code of 1997).

Donor's tax. Donor's Tax is imposed on transfer of property by way of gift at the fixed rate of 6% on total gifts in excess of PHP250,000 (approx. USD 5,000). In case a gift is made in the form of real property, the gift is valued at the higher of the fair market value as determined by the BIR commissioner, and the fair market value as determined in the schedule of values fixed by the provincial and city assessors.

Transfer tax. Local governments impose a real property transfer tax on the sale, donation, barter or any other mode of transferring the ownership or title of real property. The maximum rate is 0.5% of the total consideration, or the fair market value if the monetary consideration is not substantial, whichever is higher. Cities or municipalities within Metro Manila may impose a real property transfer tax at a maximum rate of 0.75%.

Special education fund tax. The Special Education Fund Tax is an (optional) annual tax imposed by the province or city, or a municipality within Metro Manila, at fixed rate of 1% on the assessed value of the real property. This is in addition to the RPT. The revenue is exclusively accrued to the Special Education Fund to support public education (Section 235 of the 1991 LGC).

Special levy. The Special Levy is an optional levy on lands that have specially benefited by public work projects or improvements funded by the LGU. The levy should not exceed 60% of the actual cost of the project or improvement and shall be apportioned among the affected landowners based on a computation by the *Sanggunian* (Sections 240–245 of the 1991 LGC).

Socialized housing tax. The Socialized Housing Tax is an (optional) additional levy on land, which may be imposed by LGUs at a rate of 0.5% of the assessed value of all lands in urban areas in excess of PHP50,000 (approx. USD 990), pursuant to Section 43 of Republic Act (RA) No. 7279, otherwise known as the Urban Development and Housing Act of 1992. The revenue from this tax is earmarked to fund low-cost housing projects.

Documentary stamp tax. The Documentary Stamp Tax levied on assignment, transfer or conveyance of real property at a rate of 1.5% of the consideration or value received or contracted to be paid for the realty.

---

[10]   Republic Act (RA) No. 10963, effective 1 January 2018.

Thailand

Land and building tax. The Land and Building Tax came into effect on 1 January 2020 and has replaced the former existing recurrent property taxes in Thailand: the Buildings and Land Tax (1932) and the Land Development Tax (1965). Under this law, a recurrent local property tax is levied on the appraised value of land and buildings at a differentiated, progressive tax rate depending on the usage and type of property, with some degree of local autonomy in the rate-setting. The tax is administered and collected by local authorities, and the collected tax goes directly to the local budget.

Inheritance tax. The Inheritance Tax came into effect on 1 February 2016 and is imposed on inheritances with value exceeding THB100 million (approx. USD 2.8 million). Lineal descendants and ascendants pay 5% of what they inherit, the spouse is exempt, while other heirs will be assessed at 10%. The tax is applied to the capital value of the immovable property, which is the appraised value under the Land Code deducted by the third party-rights in accordance with the criteria prescribed in Ministerial Regulations (Section 15 (1) of the Inheritance Tax Act, B.E. 2558 (2015)).

Property transfer fee. Thailand has a government fee on sale and transfer of ownership of real property. This fee is levied by the Land Department at the rate of 2% over the appraised capital value of the property as determined by the Valuation Committee and collected by local land office upon transfer of ownership (Sections 104 and 105 of the Land Code).[11]

Stamp duty tax. A stamp duty is imposed at varying rates on certain legal instruments, such as transfer of immovable property (0.5% of the sale price) and lease agreement (0.1% of total rental or any other payment under the agreement). Stamp duty is exempt if Specific Business Tax is charged on the sale of property (i.e., when property is sold within the first 5 years of ownership by certain businesses).[12]

Viet Nam

Non-agricultural land use tax. The Law on Non-Agricultural Land Use Tax was introduced in 2012 and replaced the rice productivity-based Ordinance on House and Land Tax of 1992. This recurrent property tax applies to residential, commercial, and industrial land only, with improvements and other construction on land being excluded from tax. The tax base is calculated by multiplying the taxable land area by the price per square meter as determined by the municipal or Provincial People's Committee (PPC). To this tax base, a progressive tax rate ranging 0.03%– 0.15% is applied for residential land and a flat rate of 0.03% for commercial and industrial land.[13]

Agricultural land use tax. Introduced in 1993, the Agricultural Land Use Tax is aimed at organizations and individuals that utilize land for agricultural productions. The tax is calculated based on a fixed quantity of rice per hectare and subsequently converted into money using the tariff schedule determined by the PPC. The per-hectare tax liability varies according to the land area, land class category (based on land fertility, location, topography, climate condition, and irrigation), and the type of production (annual versus long term).[14]

---

[11]   Land Code Promulgating Act, B.E. 2497 (1954), as amended until Land Code Amendment Act (No. 12), B.E. 2551 (2008).
[12]   Chapter VI of Title II of the Revenue Code.
[13]   Articles 6 and 7 of the Law on Non-Agricultural Land Use Tax.
[14]   Chapter II of the Law on Agricultural Land Use Tax.

To support farmers and encourage the development of agricultural production, a policy for exemptions and reductions to the Agricultural Land Use Tax has been implemented since 2001.[15] Under the current policy, agricultural land use tax is exempt until 31 December 2020, provided that the agricultural land area allocated by the state is directly used for agricultural production.[16] The exemption of agricultural land use tax for subjects under the current resolutions is expected to be extended for the period 2021–2025.

Registration fee. When registering land use rights and ownership of houses and other land-attached assets, the land user or owner of property on land is required to pay a registration fee (stamp duty) of 0.5% of the value of the property (with a maximum of VND500 million [approx. USD 21,500]).

Revenue Share of Taxes on Property in Asia

Taxes on property do not emerge as important sources of revenue in the four countries. In 2017, revenues from taxes on property as a percentage of GDP are highest in Cambodia (0.60%), followed by Thailand (0.49%), and

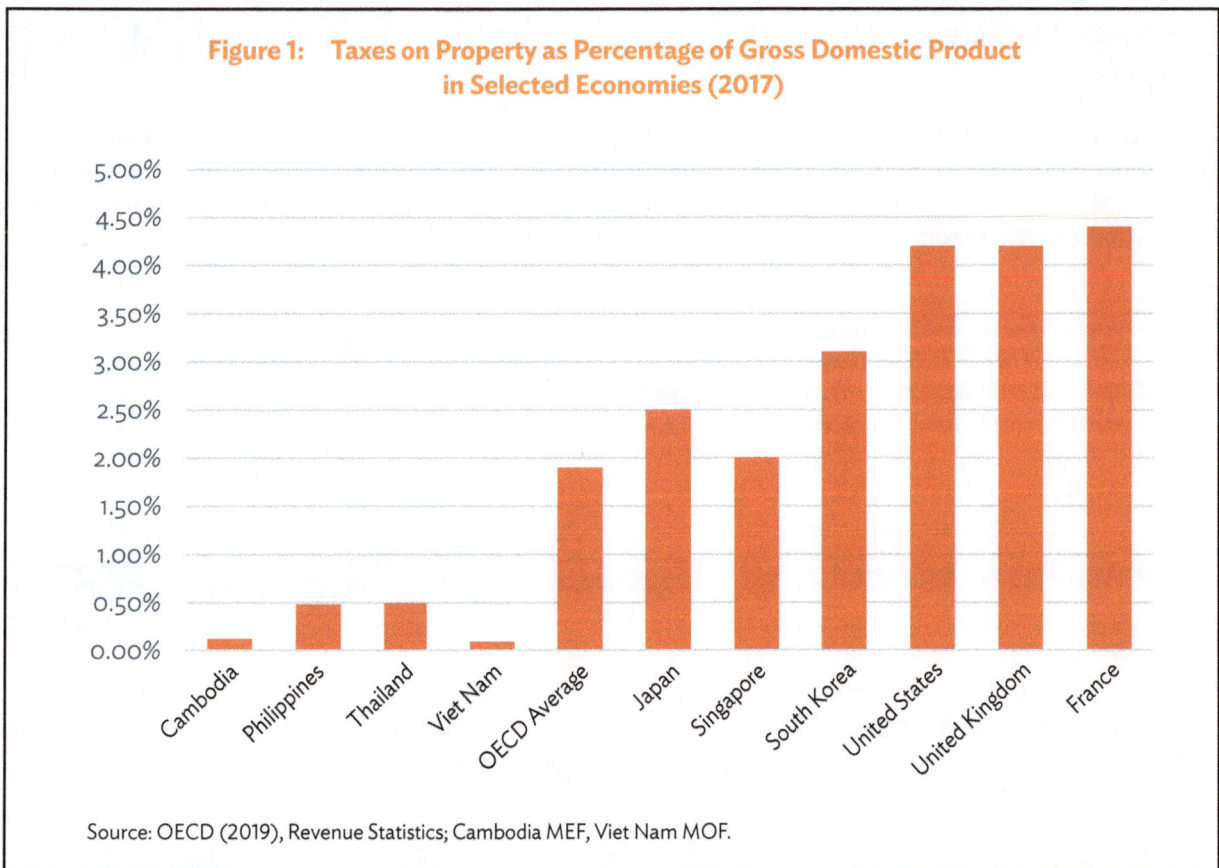

Figure 1: Taxes on Property as Percentage of Gross Domestic Product in Selected Economies (2017)

Source: OECD (2019), Revenue Statistics; Cambodia MEF, Viet Nam MOF.

---

[15] Resolution 24/1999/QH10 and Resolution 50/2001/QH10 of 29 November 2001 of the Xth National Assembly on the 2002 state budget estimates, followed by Resolution No. 15/2003/QH11 of 17 June 2003 on Agricultural Land Use Tax exemption and reduction of 17 June 2003 (and implemented by Decree No. 129/2003/ND-CP of 3 November 2003) for the period 2003–2010; and extended by Resolution 550/2010/QH12 of 24 November 2010, as amended and supplemented by Resolution 28/2016/QH14 of 11 November 2016, for the period 2011–2020.
[16] Clause 4 of Article 1, Resolution 550/2010/QH12 of 24 November 2010, as amended and supplemented by Resolution 28/2016/QH14 of 11 November 2016.

the Philippines (0.48%), with Viet Nam the lowest (0.09%). By comparison, one of the better performing countries in Asia and the Pacific, that is, the Republic of Korea, the taxes on property as percentage of GDP can reach up to 3.1%, whereas in the highest performing countries in the world (France and the United Kingdom), the tax revenues exceed 4% (see Figure 1).

From the different categories of taxes on properties, recurrent property taxes have the largest revenue share in the Philippines (79%), followed by Thailand (51%), which amount to 0.38% and 0.25% of GDP in the respective countries in 2017 (OECD 2019). By contrast, the reliance on recurrent property taxes is much lower in Cambodia and Viet Nam. Based on the revenue data provided by the Viet Nam Ministry of Finance, revenues from the agricultural land use tax and the nonagricultural land use tax combined account for only a quarter of the total revenue from taxes on property, which represent 0.024% of GDP in 2017. The lion's share of revenue from taxes on properties comes from the registration fee on land and housing. Similarly, in Cambodia, 80% of the revenues from taxes on property is derived from transfer tax for immovable property (i.e., 0.48% of GDP). Revenues from recurrent property taxes (the tax on immovable property and tax on unused land) were around 0.12% of the country's GDP in 2017. Compared with the revenue statistics in some advanced OECD economies, the performance of the recurrent property taxes in the four countries is low (see Figure 2). There is significant scope and potential for revenue improvement.

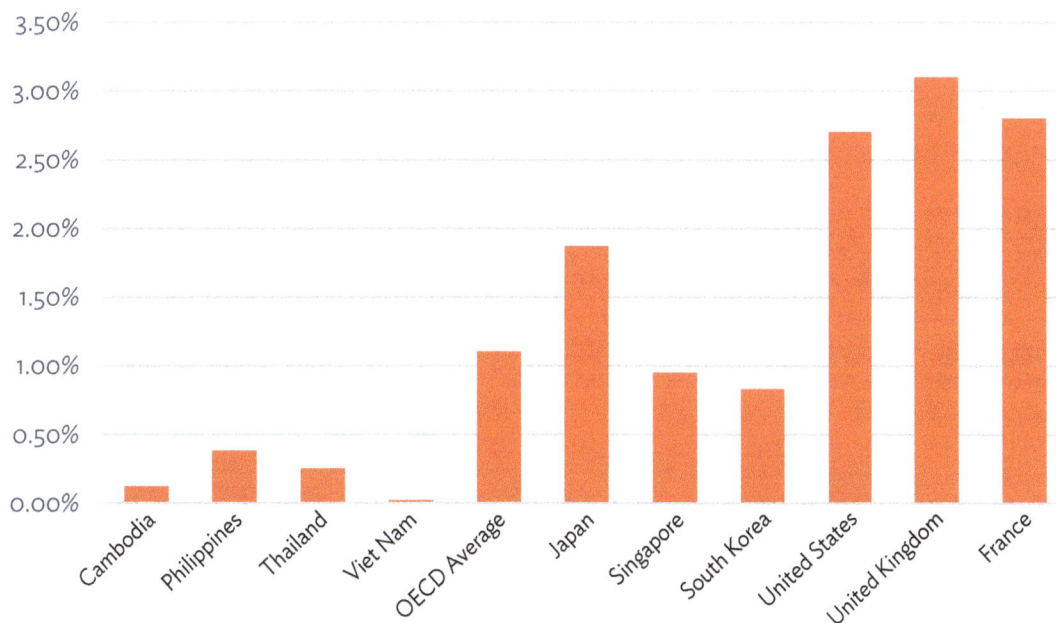

Figure 2:   Recurrent Property Tax as Percentage of Gross Domestic Product in Selected Economies (2017)

Source: OECD (2019), Revenue Statistics; Cambodia MEF, Viet Nam MOF.

For the remainder of this study, this report shall focus only on recurrent taxes on immovable property, which encompasses both "real estate" (land and any structures attached to the land) and "real property" (the rights, interests, and benefits connected with real estate), hereinafter shortened to "property tax."

Local Revenue Reliance and Intergovernmental Transfers

Consistent with international practices, revenues from property taxes in the four countries are allocated to subnational government's budget with varying degrees of local revenue autonomy, including powers over the tax base and rate-setting policies (see Chapter 4). While property tax is one of the most important tax revenue sources for local governments, it represents only a small fraction of the overall subnational budget. In most Asian and Pacific economies, subnational governments are highly dependent on intergovernmental transfers and shared revenues from national tax collection, which are often formula-based and not linked to the local tax efforts.

Cambodia

In Cambodia, the main sources of revenue for subnational administrations—the capital, province, municipality, district, *khan*, commune, and *sangkat*—are (i) local source revenue, which includes both tax and nontax revenue; (ii) national source revenue, including shared revenue and conditional and unconditional funds transferred from the national budget; and (iii) revenue from other sources as determined by law or other legal document.[17] Local source tax revenues are created for the exclusive benefit of the budget of subnational administrations[18] and includes among others, the tax on immovable property, unused land tax, and property transfer tax, which are administratively collected by the General Department of Taxation and subsequently shared among subnational levels of administration.[19] Subnational administrations do not have autonomy over these taxes, including powers over the tax base and rate-setting. According to the 2019 OECD and United Cities and Local Governments (UCLG) country report, the total revenues of all subnational administrations accounted for 1.2% of GDP (or 7.9% of general government revenue) in 2016, of which the majority share comes from tax revenues (76.5%) (OECD and UCLG 2019). Based on the data from the Ministry of Economy and Finance (MEF), revenues from the immovable property tax amounted to 0.11% of GDP and the unused land tax to 0.01%, thus in combination representing 10% of the subnational budget and 13% of the subnational tax revenue. Almost all tax revenues are allocated to the city and the provinces, of which the capital city of Phnom Penh is the largest recipient. Although some lower tiers of governments may also share in the tax revenue,[20] the communes and *sangkats* predominately rely on intergovernmental transfers through the commune and *sangkat* fund, while the districts, municipalities, and *khans* outside of Phnom Penh rely on transfers via the district municipality and *khan* fund.[21] Both funds are sourced from the central government budget according to a prescribed percentage of the national revenues from the previous year and allocated to the communes and *sangkats* the districts, municipalities, and *khans* via a formula based on population, poverty, salary, and administrative arrangements, equal shares per entity, and development spending share (footnote 21).

---

[17]   Article 24 of the 2011 Law on Regime and Property Management of Subnational Administrations (Royal Kram No. NS/RKM/0611/011).

[18]   Art. 25(1) of the 2011 Law on Regime and Property Management of Subnational Administrations (Royal Kram No. NS/RKM/0611/011).

[19]   Other subnational shared taxes are public lighting tax, accommodation tax, slaughter tax, patent and licensing tax, and means of transportation tax.

[20]   In Phnom Penh, the *sangkats* receive 20% and *khans* receive 10% of the property tax revenues allocated to the city (the remaining 70% goes to the city). As for all other provinces: the *sangkats* in the province receive 30% and 70% will go to the province.

[21]   ADB. 2018. *Fiscal Decentralization Reform in Cambodia, Progress over the past decade and opportunities*. Manila.

Philippines

In the Philippines, LGUs have a relatively high level of tax autonomy in comparison to the other three countries in this study. Provinces, cities, and municipal governments within the Metropolitan Manila area have the power to impose certain taxes, such as the RPT, business tax, real property transfer tax, special education tax, and other local levies, which are administered at the LGU level. The RPT is a major source of own revenues for LGUs; however, the fiscal performance varies greatly between the different levels of subnational governments. As shown in Figure 3, despite their taxing powers, most LGUs are highly dependent on the transfers from the national government in the form of the internal revenue allotment (IRA). The IRA is divided among different levels of local government—provinces (23%), cities (23%), municipalities (34%), and *barangays* (20%)—according to population, land area, and equal sharing, and is sourced from a predetermined share of national government revenue.[22] Currently, the IRA is calculated at 40% of the national internal revenue taxes from the third preceding fiscal year. Under the definition of "national internal revenue taxes" is understood: income tax, estate and donor's taxes, value-added tax, other percentage taxes, excise taxes, documentary stamp taxes, and such other taxes that may be imposed and collected by the BIR (Section 21 of the National Internal Revenue Code). Starting 2022, LGUs will receive a larger revenue share pursuant to a court ruling in which the Supreme Court decided that the IRA should include tax collection of other agencies apart from the BIR, such as the Bureau of Customs.

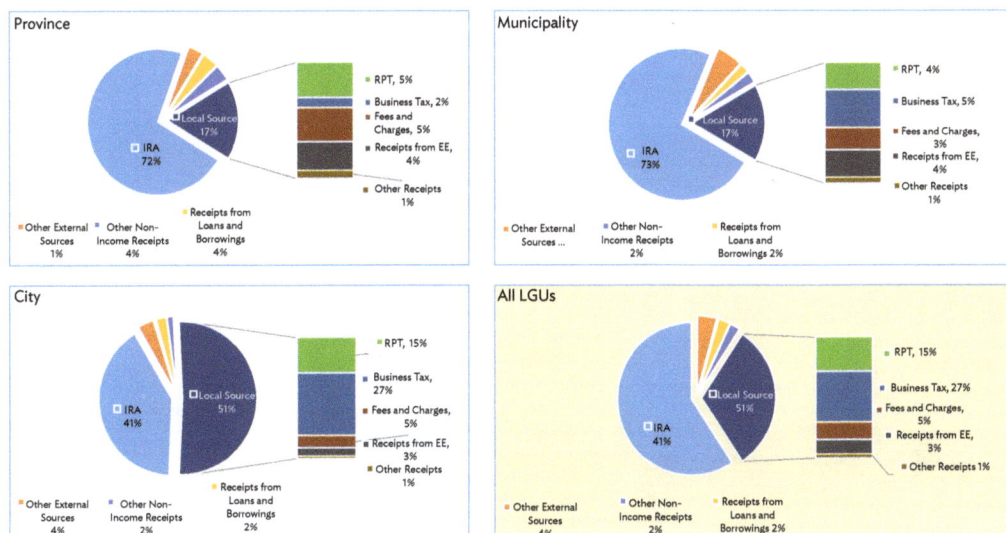

Figure 3:   Distribution of Philippines' Local Government Unit Income

Source: P.P. Quizon. 2019. *The Philippines Valuation Reform*. Presentation prepared for the ADB Conference on Property Tax Reform and Domestic Resource Mobilization in Asia and the Pacific Region. Manila. 16–18 September.

---

[22]   Section 285, Local Government Code 1991.

Thailand

The subnational government revenues in Thailand can be categorized into four sources: (i) local levy taxes, which encompass both tax and nontax revenues; (ii) shared taxes, (e.g., motor vehicle tax, mineral royalties and petroleum royalties, gambling fees, and property registration fees); (iii) surcharge taxes such as value-added tax, excise tax, and specific business tax; and (iv) conditional and nonconditional grants by the central government (subsidies). Local own source tax revenues include the land and building tax, local development tax (until 2020), signage tax, and other charges. As set out in the Determining Plan and Process of Decentralization Act 1999, the ratio of local government revenue to national government income must be at 20% by 2001 and gradually increased to 35% by 2006. This fiscal decentralization target was later lowered to 25% to be attained by 2007. In 2018, the total subnational revenue was THB636,573.20 million, representing 3.9% of GDP and reaching a ratio of 29.42% of the national government income.[23] Grants and subsidies from the central government were the largest source of income, representing 38% of local government's revenue, followed by shared taxes (34%) and surcharge taxes (18%). Local levy tax revenues accounted for only 10%, of which 54% is derived from the property taxes (the land and building tax and the local development tax). Most of the local levy tax revenues were accrued to the

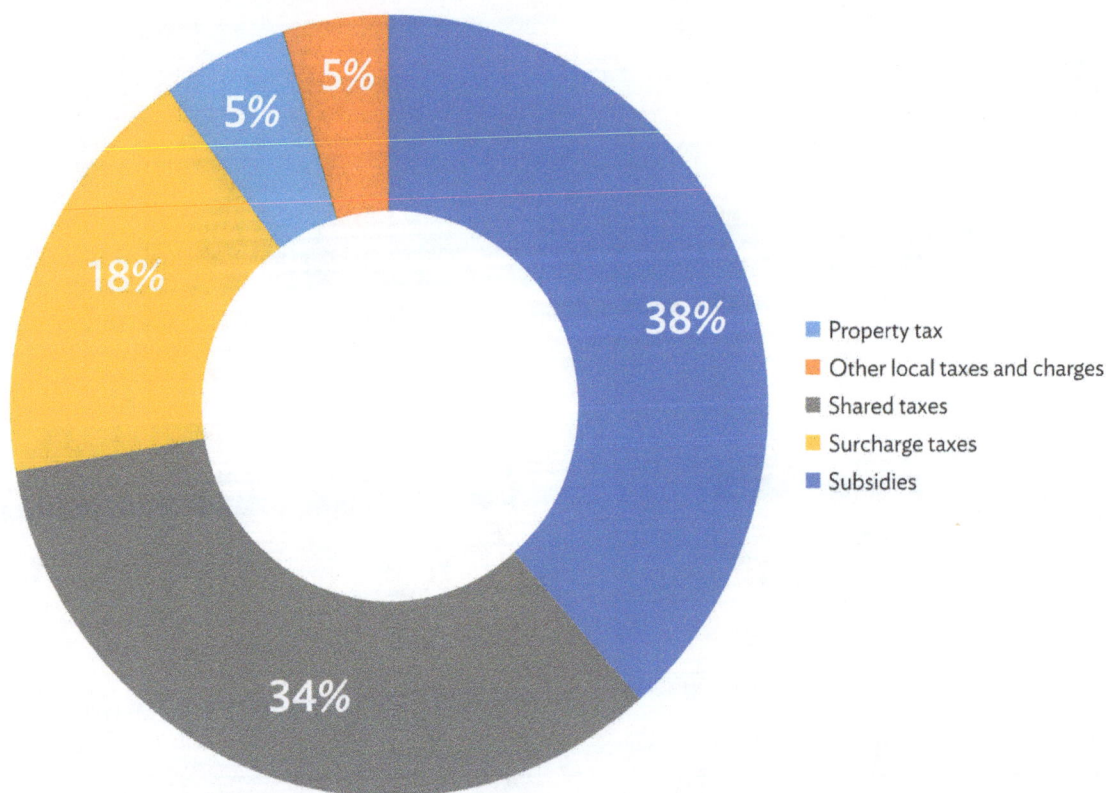

Figure 4:   Distribution of Thailand's Local Government Income in 2018

- Property tax
- Other local taxes and charges
- Shared taxes
- Surcharge taxes
- Subsidies

Source: Fiscal Policy Office of Thailand, Ministry of Finance.

---

[23]   Data from Fiscal Policy Office of Thailand, Ministry of Finance.

municipalities (39%), followed by the special organizations of Pattaya City and Bangkok (33%), the subdistricts administrative organizations (20%), and the provincial administrative organizations (9%).

Viet Nam

Viet Nam has one of the highest levels of subnational revenues in the Asia and Pacific region, representing 11.2% of GDP and 45.8% of total public revenue in 2016. A key major source of revenue for subnational governments are the fiscal transfers from the central government's budget, which account for 40% of the total subnational revenue (OECD and UCLG 2019). In Viet Nam, there are two types of intergovernmental fiscal transfer programs: unconditional balancing transfers and targeted transfers. Balancing transfers are used to reduce horizontal and vertical imbalances across districts within provinces and are calculated based on the current and estimated capital spending needs, which take into account factors such as population size, development, geographic area, and number of district administrative units (Morgan and Trinh 2016). Targeted transfers are conditional grants aimed at implementing specific national priorities (OECD and UCLG 2016, Chatry and Vincent 2019). Besides the intergovernmental transfers, subnational governments have two other main sources of revenues: (i) local taxes and fees that are wholly retained by local government budgets and (ii) shared tax revenues distributed between central government budget and local government budgets according to a "sharing rate" based on provincial fiscal capacity for each stabilization period of 3–5 years as determined by the National Assembly. These revenues are collected by General Department of Taxation, operating under the Ministry of Finance, with offices at the provincial and district levels; local government administrations have little to no autonomy over tax policy and administration. Property taxes and other locally assigned taxes and levies as listed under Article 37 of the Law on State Budget 2015 (e.g., severance tax, license tax, land levies, registration fee) constitute a relatively small share of subnational government's budget. The majority of tax receipts comes from shared taxes such as value-added tax (except on imported goods), corporate income tax, personal income tax, special excise tax, and environmental protection tax.[24] To promote revenue collection, Viet Nam's budget law stipulates that local authorities are allowed to retain up to 30% of the additional collected shared taxes in excess of the budgeted amount (OECD and UCLG 2016, Chatry and Vincent 2019).

Summary

The four countries in this study all have some type of recurrent taxes on immovable property in place, often more than one. Until recently, Thailand had an annual tax on commercial properties (the 1932 Buildings and Land Tax) and on undeveloped land (the 1965 Land Development Tax). Effective 1 January 2020, these taxes were merged and replaced by a single, recurrent property tax: The Land and Building Tax. Both Cambodia and the Philippines have, besides their more traditional property tax regime, a separate recurrent tax for unused or vacant land. Viet Nam does not have a property tax in the modern sense of the term, but a recurrent land use tax for agricultural land and for nonagricultural land. As shown in Figure 2, recurrent property taxes do not emerge as an important source of revenue in the four countries, with the highest reported revenue yield of 0.38% of GDP in the Philippines, and the lowest in Viet Nam with only 0.024% of GDP in 2017.

---

[24]   Articles 37(2) and 35(2) of the Law on State Budget 2015 (No. 83/2015/QH13).

Consistent with international practices, revenues from property taxes in the four countries are allocated to subnational governments' budget, with varying degrees of local revenue autonomy. In the Philippines and Thailand, the property tax is an own-source revenue for subnational governments, levied and administered at the local level and over which local authorities have been assigned taxing powers, including power over the tax rates within certain boundaries. In Cambodia and Viet Nam, property taxes are administered and enforced by the General Department of Taxation, operating under the Ministry of Finance; local government administrations have little to no autonomy over tax policy and administration.

While property tax is one of the most important tax revenue sources for local governments, it represents a small fraction of the overall subnational budget. In 2016, property taxes accounted for around 10% of Cambodia's subnational budget. In the Philippines, the RPT is a major source of income for LGUs; however, the fiscal performance varies greatly between the different levels of subnational governments, ranging from 5% in the provinces, 4% in the municipalities, and 15% in the cities, with an average of 9% for all LGUs. In Thailand, the building and land tax and the land development tax combined accounted for only 5% of subnational resources in 2018, while Viet Nam's land use taxes are insignificant in revenue terms. Intergovernmental transfers and central government's grants and subsidies remain in most cases the mainstay of subnational income, which are often formula-based and not linked to the local tax mobilization efforts.

III. Property Tax Refrorm: Rationales and Benchmark of Strategies

Introduction

This chapter describes the primary rationales for initiating property tax reform; the current issues regarding the property tax system in Cambodia, the Philippines, Thailand, and Viet Nam; and subsequently, the different reform strategies deployed or under consideration in the four countries to address those issues.

According to Rosengard, there are generally four primary rationales for initiating property tax reform in a country, that is, to improve (i) revenue for government, (ii) social equity, (iii) economic efficiency, and/or (iv) administrative cost-effectiveness (Rosengard 2013, with reference to Muellbauer 2005).

Improving Revenue Performance

Raising revenue is the most common rationale for property tax reform (Von Haldenwang 2015) and attempts thereto are numerous and widespread, but often unsuccessful (Martinez-Vazquez et al. 2010). According to Rosengard, there are three key dimensions of policy pitfalls in designing and implementing property tax reform: political, technical, and tactical. Political challenge can be both internal (e.g., the reform is "sabotaged" through delayed, slow or incorrect administration) and external (e.g., resistance by the rich and powerful). Most prevalent technical shortcomings are (i) lack of reliable data, often resulting in inaccurate revenue forecasting and unintended policy outcomes, and (ii) insufficient financial and human resources, contributing to inadequate administrative capacity for effective implementation of the reform. The third policy pitfall is tactical, revolving around the strategic timing and sequencing of property tax reform (Rosengard 2013).

It has been argued that moving toward fiscal decentralization would increase property tax revenue mobilization in developing countries (Bahl and Martinez-Vazquez 2008). Martinez-Vazquez, Noiset, and Rider empirically tested this hypothesis and concluded that this is true in developed countries, but not in low-income, developing countries. Weak administration is the most important obstacle for property tax revenue mobilization in developing countries. While the authors believe that the property tax should be a mainstay of local government financing, keeping the administration of the property tax at the central government level until the local administrative capacity is better developed would improve the tax's revenue performance (Martinez-Vazquez et al. 2010). Central administration would also have the advantages of economies of scale, uniformity in assessment, and collection practices. In addition, the central government might be better equipped to engage in a more balanced fight with powerful local elites in tax disputes (Mikesell 2013).

Improving Social Equity

Property tax is considered equitable. It has been argued that property tax is fair because those owning property of the same value, or paying the same property rent, are subject to the same tax (horizontal equity) (Bahl 2009). Property tax can also be used as a policy instrument for income redistribution, although the distributional effect of property tax is heavily influenced by the policy choices on the tax base, tax rate, and valuation, as well as by the administration and enforcement of the tax. As property ownership is heavily concentrated among the wealthy in developing countries, and low-valued properties and public housing are generally not taxed at all, property tax can be progressive. If properly designed and administered, the tax burden can predominantly rest on the middle- and high-income earners. Property taxes can thus promote vertical equity, where individuals with higher ability to pay are paying a larger part of the tax burden as a proportion of their income.

The objective of treating equals equally (horizontal equity) and unequals unequally (vertical equity), however, may be difficult to fully achieve. It is hard to measure the distributional effects of property taxes in low-income, developing countries where compliance and governance is weak and relevant statistics are few and sometimes inaccurate. The effectiveness of property tax as a policy instrument for income redistribution purposes is reduced under these circumstances and there may be other more effective and better-suited tools available to achieving these objectives. While property tax is generally considered a fair tax, there is no direct link between tax liability and the ability to pay. It is clear that many who are property rich will also be rich in financial capital and are able to pay, but some taxpayers may be "asset rich but cash poor" at certain times in their lives, for example, elderly taxpayers who may have exhausted their retirement savings. Horizontal and vertical equity can also be compromised by assessment practices, exemption policies, and weak enforcement.

Property tax equity can be improved by introducing policy changes on base definitions, tax rate structures, and/or tax relief measures for poor and cash-strapped households (e.g., tax deferral schemes) to ensure horizontal and vertical equity, based on the benefit or ability to pay principles. Equity can also be achieved through improved administration and enforcement, which ensures that assessments and, ultimately, taxes are distributed as equitably and fairly as possible under the law. Completeness of the fiscal cadastre or tax roll, uniformity in valuation and assessment practices, frequency in updating, and effectiveness of appeals mechanism are critical elements in the administration process.

Improving Economic Efficiency

Property tax is considered one of the most efficient forms of taxation and the least harmful to long-term economic growth. However, depending on its design, property taxation can distort economic choices or behavior, which may or may not be intentional. For instance, property taxation may influence consumer's choice on buying or renting; it might also affect capital spending on property improvements, as it would result in higher taxes due to value increase. Similarly, property taxation might also induce tax competition between municipalities due to the differences in tax rates and service levels across local jurisdictions. Minimizing the distortional impact of property taxation on the production and consumption decisions is the third primary rationale for initiating reform.

According to Kelly, property tax efficiency can be enhanced by introducing policy changes to minimize exemptions to ensure a broader property tax base and by establishing higher tax rates on vacant, undeveloped land (Kelly 2013). Adopting a uniform rate structure can also contribute to efficiency of the system, as different types of properties are taxed the same, hence limiting the risk of tax-induced distortions.

Improving Administrative Cost-Effectiveness

One of the most common explanations for the poor revenue performance of property tax in developing, low-income countries is that the tax is administered inefficiently due to , for example, the complexity of the tax system, lack of administrative capacity and technical expertise, and the absence of a full and up-to-date cadastre and reliable data on sales prices (Bird and Slack 2002). Even when a property tax is well administered, it will not come off as a relatively efficient revenue producer due to the high administrative costs related to property identification, assessment, and valuation, and the development and maintenance of a comprehensive and accurate fiscal cadastre or tax registry.

Ways to improve administrative cost-effectiveness include simplification (e.g., revising policy choices on tax base, rate structure, and exemption policy); standardization (e.g., unified record keeping, uniform assessment, and valuation practices); and automation of property taxation. New technologies such as computer-assisted mass appraisal (CAMA) system with geographic information system (GIS), satellite-aided mapping, and cross-referencing data between intergovernmental agencies can also improve the way countries administer their property taxes.

The four countries in this study are at different stages of reform but share the common objective of improving the revenue performance of the property tax regime.

Property Tax Reform in Cambodia

Current Issues

In Cambodia, the current property tax revenues are very low. Based on the MEF 2019 revenue target, the immovable property tax is expected to yield US$27.8 million, reaching about 0.10% of GDP.[25]

Like most property taxes, the Tax on Immovable Property is a local government tax allocated, to the subnational government (cities, provinces, towns, districts, *khans*, communes, and *sangkats*) for its regional development. The tax, however, has not yet become a significant revenue producer for Cambodia because of a combination of both policy design and administrative issues. For a start, the statutory tax rate is low, and the scope of tax is limited to only properties located in the capital city of Phnom Penh and in the cities of the provinces. In addition, a large number of properties, in particular those in the provinces, is exempted from the tax. Furthermore, the tax base for the immovable property tax is not based on the full market value, but 80% of the assessed market value minus a general exemption of KHR100 million (approx. USD 25,000). Besides the low rate and narrow tax base, difficulties to include all properties in the tax roll have also contributed to the poor revenue performance of the Tax on Immovable Property (Fung and McAuley 2020). As the fiscal cadastre is person-based,[26] the system depends largely on taxpayers to register the property by submitting accurate declarations of their property holdings and supporting documents (PT01 form), to file the property tax return (PT02 form), to calculate their tax liability and pay the tax annually at the local tax administration where the property is located by 30 September. When registering the property, taxpayers are given a property identification number (PIN). However, cases of issuing two or more PINs on one property or wrongful filing (e.g., under reporting on the size of property or appraisal valuation,

---

[25]   Ministry of Economy and Finance, Budget Law 2019.
[26]   A fiscal cadastre can either be person (or taxpayer) based or property (or map) based. A person-based cadastre lists the persons, both physical and legal, and information about the properties they are known to possess. By contrast, a property-based cadastre is organized by property, which holds information on the location, zoning, and the owners and/or users.

nonreporting on changes in merging or splitting of land and other modification of properties) and nonfiling of tax returns by taxpayers, are not uncommon. Furthermore, fragmented and incomplete data keeping, as well as lack of coordination between government institutions responsible for the registration and maintaining property records further complicate the government's efforts to improve the coverage ratio of the property tax.

Another determinant of revenue performance of the property tax is the valuation. A property tax system, based on assessed market values, depends on the presence of a transparent and active real estate market, which offers a source of accurate transaction data as a basis for an objective assessment of the market value of all types of real property in all locations. In Cambodia, the property market is considered immature and developing. The land tenure and titling system has yet to be fully developed to the point where full transparency and security of the titles of land ownership are ensured. Real estate sales and transactions are believed to be often under reported to evade the 4% transfer tax. As such, reliable data on recent sales and listing prices are not readily available in Cambodia to provide accurate market value assessments (Fung and McAuley 2020).

Reform Strategy

Cambodia has previously stated its policy under the Revenue Mobilization Strategy 2014–2018 to increase domestic resource mobilization by improving revenue administration and tax collection with better skills and systems, and not by adding new taxes or increasing tax rates. As such, the current property tax reform is mainly an administrative one, with a focus on improving the registration and valuation of properties in the tax roll while strengthening enforcement and compliance. The reform measures include (i) gaining improved access to property information from the General Department of Cadastre and Geography of the Ministry of Land Management Urban Planning and Construction (MLMUPC), (ii) conducting periodic surveys by trained property assessors to increase the amount of properties registered in the tax system and to update the existing property information in the database, and (iii) updating the property values in the tax roll (Fung and McAuley 2020).

Cambodia recently completed a revaluation of properties. Effective 1 July 2019, property base values for the purpose of transfer tax have been revised and increased across the country. In some potential urban areas, the increase was 70%–80% of the market value. For the levy of the property tax, the reappraisal is expected to create a significant tax hike (in some cases an increase of 100%). To make the reform politically more palatable and to address the concerns of "asset rich and cash poor" households, the government of Cambodia is carrying out a study on the policy options to dampen the impact of tax increase, which include an adjustment of the tax base value or the base exemption. It is also proposed that properties shall be reappraised at least every 5 years (Fung and McAuley 2020).

To ensure the success of the administrative reform, Cambodia is developing a set of key performance indicators and targets under the Revenue Mobilization Strategy 2019–2023 to monitor the implementation and results of the ongoing reform efforts. Under the new strategy, the government is also considering expanding the scope of the property tax to downtown areas (mainly districts) and to review the existing exemption policies. In addition, the government is currently conducting a study to enact a legislation that will provide the tax administration full powers to obtain information and data from relevant government institutions for tax purposes (Fung and McAuley 2020).

Property Tax Reform in the Philippines

Current Issues

Under the LGC 1991, an LGU can impose a tax on real property based on the assessed value of the property. LGUs exercise significant control over the valuation of properties; however, factors such as weak institutional local capacities, limited access to critical data, and sparse use of information technologies have resulted in distorted real property values. In addition, political interventions in property valuation created conflicting incentives for local officials, which prevent them from maximizing revenues to finance local service delivery.[27] Over the last 3 years, only 37% of LGUs have updated the schedule of market values (SMVs).[28] Apart from the large regional disparities in property valuation, the outdated SMVs also adversely impacted the revenue performance of the RPT, which currently stands at 0.36% of GDP. According to the Department of Finance, provinces and cities are losing an estimated PHP 30.5 billion (approx. USD 581.5 million) in forgone revenues.[29]

Reform Strategy

With the aim to professionalize the real property valuation system, as well as to broaden the tax base without raising tax rates, the proposed Real Property Valuation and Assessment Reform Act (House Bill No. 4664)[30] under Package 3 of the Comprehensive Tax Reform Program seeks the following:

- Adopt internationally accepted real property valuation standards.

- Establish a single property valuation based on true market values for tax purposes through the adoption of uniform SMVs.

- Depoliticize the valuation process by recentralizing the approval of the SMVs by the local *Sanggunian* back to the secretary of the Department of Finance, with review functions of the Bureau of Local Government Finance (BLGF), in coordination with the Bureau of Internal Revenue. LGUs, however, remain responsible for setting, adjusting, and regulating the tax rates and assessment levels.

- Strengthen BLGF's functions of oversight and technical support to LGUs on property valuation and assessment.

Once signed into law, this bill will boost the tax collection of the RPT, real property transfer taxes, and other property-related taxes. For the RPT, the tax-to-GDP ratio is expected to rise from 0.36% to 0.43%, while its revenue share to local income will increase to 23%.[31]

On 25 November 2019, the House of Representatives passed the Real Property Valuation and Assessment Reform Act on its third and final reading. At the time of writing this report, the bill was still pending with the Ways and Means Committee of the Senate (since 27 November 2019).[32]

---

[27] ADB. 2018. *Valuation reform project concept note brief.* No. PHI 52173-001. Manila.
[28] Government of the Philippines, Department of Finance. 2019. *Package 3: Real property valuation reform.* http://taxreform.dof.gov.ph/presentations-and-references/ctrp-package-3-real-property-valuation-reform-1-page-briefer/ (last visited on 26 February 2020).
[29] Government of the Philippines, Department of Finance. 2019. *LGUs losing P30.5-B revenues to outdated real property valuation.* http://taxreform.dof.gov.ph/news_and_updates/lgus-losing-p30-5-b-revenues-to-outdated-real-property-valuation/(accessed on 26 February 2020) .
[30] Government of the Philippines, Department of Finance. 2020. *House Bill No. 4664: Real property valuation (18th Congress).* https://taxreform.dof.gov.ph/presentations-and-references/house-bill-no-4664-real-property-valuation-18th-congress/ (accessed on 26 February 2020).
[31] Footnote 30, under benefits of the reform.
[32] Footnote 30, under legislative status.

In addition, the Philippines is currently considering other property-related tax reform proposals such as (i) the introduction of a national betterment levy (see Section 1.2); (ii) the adjustment of the zero-rate assessment levels on buildings and structures based on inflation rates and current prices; (iii) the enactment of a land trust law that allows private landowners on which infrastructure will be built to continue owning their property in exchange for an annual income stream equivalent to rent for the landowner; (iv) improving the enforcement of the Idle Land Tax to regulate land banking and speculation, while encouraging land development and promoting responsible property ownership and management; and (v) reforming the local transfer tax by succession (e.g., adjusting the period required to settle the tax.) (footnote 7).

Property Tax Reform in Thailand

Thailand has recently enacted the Land and Building Tax Act, which entered into force on 1 January 2020. The new law, which was initially proposed in 1995 (Varanyuwatana 2004), revokes and replaces the Buildings and Land Tax Act B.E. 2475 (1932) and the Land Development Tax B.E. 2508 (1965). The rationales for reform are (i) to increase tax revenue, as the replaced recurrent property taxes did not significantly contribute to local government revenue (approx. 0.2% of GDP); (ii) to enhance property tax administration and taxpayer compliance by merging the two taxes; (iii) increase land utilization; (iv) promote fiscal decentralization; and (v) increase autonomy and transparency of local administration (Boonyanate 2019).

The new tax is expected to increase the property tax revenue by 17%, from the current THB34 billion (2018) to THB40 billion, after a phase-in period of 3 years.

Issues with the Revoked Taxes

Buildings and Land Tax

The 1932 Buildings and Land Tax was levied on the owners of a house, building structure, or land that is rented or otherwise put to commercial use, on an annual basis at a rate of 12.5% of the actual or assessed annual rental value of the property, whichever is higher. The owners had to declare the rental values annually. Royal palaces, properties of government and state enterprises that are used for public activities, and religious properties were exempted, as were residential buildings occupied by owners and buildings unoccupied for a consecutive period of 12 months or longer. A reduced tax rate applied for factories and dwellings to which machinery has been attached to encourage manufacturing investments.

Two of the main issues of this tax was its tax base duplication with income tax (Boonyanate 2019) and the exemption of owner-occupied residential buildings. The latter narrowed the tax base significantly and reduced the social equity effect of the tax since it provided greater benefits to the wealthier, who own a large plot of land and a grand house. It also created administrative challenges in determining whether or not buildings were actually used for residential purposes. In a similar vein, the exemption for unoccupied buildings was difficult to verify. As there is no standard "annual rental value" for the tax base, the system relied on self-declaration by taxpayers, which was then judged based on the discretion of the officers, with risks of under declaration and rent-seeking. In addition, the Thai government did not have in place the monitoring and implementation measures it needed to enforce the law effectively. Moreover, the tax rate of the Building and Land Tax created an incentive for tax evasion, while the fees and penalty assessed for tax evasion were low and did not serve as a meaningful deterrent (Laovakul 2016).

Land Development Tax

The annual Local Development Tax was imposed on the person owning or possessing land, with the rate depending on the location and the appraised value of the property, as assessed by the local authorities. The tax was a fixed amount THB per *rai* (a *rai* is equivalent to 1,600 square meters (m^2) on a progressive scale. The implicit rates, however, were regressive: if the appraised value of land was less than THB30,000 per *rai* (approx. USD 1010), the average tax rate was 0.5%, but when the value was more than THB30,000 per rai (approx. USD 1010), the tax rate was only 0.25%. Thus, lands of lower value were taxed more heavily. Idle land was charged at twice the normal rate, while land used for annual crops was charged at half the rate, with landowners doing their own farming being subjected to a low maximum rate. Land owned or used by the government and religious institutions were exempted from tax, as were residential land and land used for cultivation, subject to certain maximum areas. Like the Land and Building Tax, the tax base of the Local Development Tax was narrow due to the exemption of residential properties. In addition, the tax was based on outdated assessed value of land from the years 1978–1981 (Laovakul 2016).

The New Land and Building Tax

The new Land and Building Tax replaces the previously mentioned recurrent property taxes and is expected to increase tax revenue and to enhance administration and taxpayer compliance. One of the significant changes under the new law is the inclusion of residential properties in the tax base. A base exemption of THB50 million (approx. USD 1.6 million) applies to residential land and building that serves as the primary residence for the individual property owner, and an exemption of THB10 million (approx. USD 325,000) for residential buildings only. Second homes are fully taxed. Furthermore, the property tax has a progressive tax rate structure, with higher rates for unutilized land, which will increase over time if left unused. The assessment base is the total appraised value of property (including both buildings and land) as set by the Treasury Department, instead of rental value, which will address one of the main administrative problems of the 1932 Buildings and Land Tax. To improve the administration of the tax, the government is developing a new centralized property tax database, in which the data from the Department of Lands (cadastre) will be enhanced with property values from the Treasury Department and provided in a template for local government offices to add their local tax information. For detailed information on the design features and policy elements of the Land and Building Tax, see Chapter 4.

Property Tax Reform in Viet Nam

Current Issues

There are currently two recurrent property taxes in place in Viet Nam: the 1993 Agricultural land use tax and the 2012 Non-Agricultural Land Use Tax. As a source of revenue, the share of both taxes in Viet Nam's total tax receipt is very low. According to data provided by the Ministry of Finance, revenues from the Agricultural Land Use Tax and the Non-Agricultural Land Use Tax together yielded around 0.024% of the country's GDP in 2017. The low revenue performance can be contributed to the narrow tax base (land only), extensive list of tax exemptions and reductions, and low valuations. For detailed information on the design features and policy elements of the Agricultural Land Use Tax and the Non-Agricultural Land Use Tax, see Chapter 4.

Reform Strategy

As set out in Viet Nam's Sustainable Development Strategy for 2011–2020, enhancing the performance of taxes is instrumental to fulfilling the targets for sustainable development set by the National Assembly.[33] Accordingly, the Ministry of Finance proposed in 2018 a tax on houses. In its initial proposal, the draft Law on Property Tax would replace the current Agricultural land use tax and the Non-Agricultural Land Use Tax and impose a tax on both land and buildings. The objectives for reform were to (i) strengthen Viet Nam's institutional capacity to generate additional resources for reinvestment in lands and marginal re-distribution of incomes for social equity; (ii) dis-incentivize speculation in residential houses and land, subsequently improving access to (affordable) real estate market for the people; (iii) promote efficient use of land; and (iv) simplify the legal framework by consolidating the existing two taxes. The proposal was subsequently sent to ministries, branches, localities, organizations, and individuals in society in accordance with the Law on promulgation of legal documents before submitting it to the government and the National Assembly for consideration and approval.[34] However, following the government's direction, the Ministry of Finance has resumed its comprehensive property tax reform study and will, in the light thereof, amend and supplement the original proposal accordingly under the new Housing and Land Tax at an appropriate time.

Summary

As set out by Rosengard (Rosengard 2013, with reference to Muellbauer 2005), property tax reform generally serves one or more of the following objectives:

1. Raising revenue for government to fund public goods and services;

2. Improving social equity by assuring a fair tax burden distribution among taxpayers;

3. Enhancing economic efficiency by minimizing the distortional impact of the property tax on economic behavior; and

4. Improving the administrative cost-effectiveness of the tax system through simplification, standardization, and automation.

The four countries in this study have each adopted different strategies and are at varying stages of reform, but they all share the common principal objective of improving the revenue performance of the property tax regime. Both Viet Nam and Thailand have undertaken a comprehensive approach to overhaul the property tax system by replacing and merging the existing taxes and moving toward a modern property tax. While Viet Nam is carrying out a comprehensive property tax reform study, Thailand's new Land and Building Tax came into effect on 1 January 2020. Cambodia's reform is primarily focused on improving the property tax administration by expanding the tax base coverage, increasing the valuation level, and strengthening the enforcement and compliance measures, while conducting further studies to improve social equity and raising more revenue. The Philippines has the most decentralized property tax system of the jurisdictions targeted in this study; however, local disparities in property valuation have affected the revenue performance of the RPT. The Philippines' Real Property Valuation and Assessment Reform Act aims to improve the quality and uniformity of the real property valuation system and the bill has advanced to the final stages of the legislative process.

---

[33] Government of Viet Nam. *Viet Nam Sustainable Development Strategy for 2011–2020.* Ha Noi. http://www.vietnam.gov.vn/portal/page/portal/English/strategies/strategiesdetails?categoryId=30&articleId=10050825.

[34] Official Letter No. 4294/BTC-CST dated April 13, 2018, of the Ministry of Finance.

Table 3 provides an overview of the reform strategies and the primary rationales behind the initiatives, which may serve as a benchmark to monitor progress on the ongoing reforms.

Table 3:   Benchmark of Reform Strategies

Primary Rationales	Reform Strategy			
	Cambodia	Philippines	Thailand	Viet Nam
Revenue raising	Strengthening enforcement and compliance Updating property values to 70%–80% of market value Mandating frequent revaluations (every 5 years) Updating property registration and database Expanding coverage area of the tax	Proposed Real Property Valuation and Assessment Reform Act to improve the quality of real property valuation and to broaden the tax base Expected RPT-revenue increase to 0.43% of GDP	Enacted new Land and Building Tax (2020) to broaden tax base, enhance administration, and taxpayer compliance Adopted appraised market value (instead of rental value) Expected revenue increase by 17% after a 3-year phase-in period	Considering adopting a modern value-based property tax regime Broadening tax base by taxing both land and improvements (instead of land-only)
Social equity	Developing tax relief measures to cushion impact of tax increase Exemption policies for "asset rich and cash poor"		Progressive tax rate structure Inclusion of high value owner-occupied residential properties in the tax base Transitional provisions to mitigate impact of tax reform	Exemption policies for "asset rich and cash poor"
Economic efficiency		Promoting efficient land use through better enforcement and collection of the Idle Land Tax	Establishing higher rates on unutilized or vacant land to stimulate efficient land use	
Administrative cost-effectiveness	Improving intergovernmental data exchange and access to property-related information for tax purposes	Standardizing of valuation process Establishing single valuation base for taxation Adopting international standards Recentralize and depoliticize the approval of SMVs Establishing an electronic database to support valuation	Simplifying legal framework by merging 2 taxes Developing a centralized property tax database	Simplifying legal framework by merging 2 land use taxes

RPT = real property tax, SMV = schedule of market values.
Source: Authors' analysis based on information provided by the General Department of Taxation (GDT) of Cambodia, Bureau of Local Government Finance (BLGF) of the Philippines, Fiscal Policy Office (FPO) of Thailand, and Ministry of Finance of Viet Nam.

IV. Main Design Features of Property Taxation

Introduction

The ability of a property tax to meet its objectives and strategic goals depends to a large extent on the characteristics of the tax (policy design and administration), whether those objectives and goals are to raise domestic revenue to meet the Sustainable Development Goals, to capture land value, to promote efficient land use, to stabilize residential property prices, to support fiscal decentralization, or otherwise. However, the available policy options for countries to choose from may be quite different. Culture, demographics, socioeconomic developments, institutional framework, and other country-specific characteristics define a country's practical options for policy design and implementation. The level of local autonomy and fiscal decentralization, the rate of urbanization and development, the distribution of wealth or level of income inequality, and so on may also have implications for tax policy.

This chapter focuses on the key policy design features of property taxation: tax subject, tax base, tax rate, and property valuation.

Tax Subject

Property tax laws typically define the person or entity liable to tax (the tax subject) as follows: (i) the owner, (ii) the occupant or user, (iii) the property itself regardless of who owns or uses it, or (iv) some combination of the aforementioned. The choice depends on a variety of factors, such as the status of private property ownership rights in a country, but also practical and administrative considerations.

In Viet Nam, where land ownership rights are collective and the state may only grant land use rights to individuals, households, and organizations for different periods of time, the subject of the property taxes (i.e., the Non-Agricultural Land Use Tax and the Agricultural Land Use Tax Law) logically follows the occupant or user of land. In Thailand, persons subject to tax are individuals and juristic persons owning land or buildings (or, in the case of government-owned properties, those who have possessory rights thereof). As there are generally more property occupants than there are property owners, limiting the liability for the property tax to only the owners reduces not only the number of taxpayers in the system, but arguably also the costs of administration, appeals, and enforcement.

Both the Philippines and Cambodia have a broader definition of the tax subject. In Cambodia, the Tax on Immovable Property can be collected from the owner, the occupier, or the final beneficiary of the property. In the Philippines, the RPT is a tax on the property itself and remains attached to the property until paid (Miranda 2019). It shall, however, be the responsibility of the real property owner (natural or juridical person) or administrator to declare the current and fair market value of the property with the local authorities. If such owner or administrator fails to

Table 4:   Tax Subjects

Country	Name of Instrument	Tax Subject			
		Owner	Occupant or User	Property Itself	Other
Cambodia	Tax on Immovable Property	✓	✓		✓
	Tax on Unused Land	✓	✓		✓
Philippines	Real Property Tax	✓	✓	✓	✓
	Idle Land Tax	✓	✓	✓	✓
Thailand	Land and Building Tax	✓	✓*		
Viet Nam	Non-Agricultural Land Use Tax		✓		
	Agricultural Land Use Tax		✓		

* In the case of government-owned properties.
Source: Authors' analysis based on analysis of the listed legal instruments.

make a declaration within the prescribed time, the provincial or city assessor can declare the property on behalf of the defaulting owner and assess the property in accordance with the law.

The choice of tax subject in the four countries is summarized in Table 4.

Tax Base

Property taxes are generally levied on all types of immovable properties: residential, commercial, and industrial and well as on agricultural properties (although the different categories of properties may be treated differently). The term "immovable property" is commonly understood to mean land or any permanent structure above or below the surface that cannot be moved without destroying or altering it. This term, however, does not necessarily correlate with the tax base definition of property taxes used in subnational laws.

The choice of tax base varies from country to country. Some countries tax land only (also known as "site value taxation"). Viet Nam, for example, taxes the different types of lands (agricultural land under the Agricultural Land Use Tax; residential, commercial, and industrial land under the Non-Agricultural Land Use Tax), but does not include improvements and other constructions on land in its tax bases. According to Bird and Slack, taxation of land only scores well in terms of both efficiency and equity. Since improvements to land are not taxed, land taxes are neutral in terms of development decisions (in contrast to a property tax on land and buildings that discourages investments in property). If the effective tax on land is high, land use will be more efficient as speculation or hoarding of land would become economically less attractive. In addition, as land is fixed in supply and landownership is unequally distributed, it has been argued that site value taxation would be more progressive than a tax on both land and improvements. In terms of the administration of the tax, it has also been argued that land taxes are easier and cheaper to administer because cadastral recordkeeping is simpler. In practice, most countries tax both land and improvements, in part due to the administrative difficulties in assessing separate values. Furthermore, considering its narrow base, site value taxation is likely to produce lower revenues (Bird and Slack 2004). Viet Nam is considering to replace both the agricultural and non-Agricultural Land Use Taxes with a single property tax and move from a land-only tax to taxing both land and buildings.

Table 5:   Tax Base

Country	Name of Instrument	Tax Object			
		Land	Building	Intangibles	Movables
Cambodia	Tax on Immovable Property	✓	✓		
	Tax on Unused Land	✓	✓		
Philippines	Real Property Tax	✓	✓	✓	✓
	Idle Land Tax	✓			
Thailand	Land and Building Tax	✓	✓	✓	
Viet Nam	Non-Agricultural Land Use Tax	✓			
	Agricultural Land Use Tax	✓			

Source: Authors, based on an analysis of the legal instruments.

Most countries tax both lands and improvements. In Cambodia, the tax base is immovable property, which is defined to include land, houses, buildings, and other construction that are built on that land under the Tax on Immovable Property. However, the scope is limited to properties located in the capital city of Phnom Penh and in the cities of the provinces. Under the Tax on Used Land, the tax base is unused land, including unused land with existing buildings in an abandoned state. In Thailand, in addition to land and buildings, the tax base also includes possessory rights over government-owned land and buildings. Of the four countries, the Philippines has the broadest tax base, which is defined as all the rights, interests, and benefits related to the ownership of "real estate." (i.e., the land and all those items that are attached to the land, either permanently or temporarily, such as buildings, machinery, and other improvements. It is the physical, tangible entity, together with all the additions or improvements on, above or below the ground,[35] including natural resources in their original state.)

The choice of tax base in the four countries is summarized in Table 5.

Tax Rate

The structure and level of property tax rates vary across and even within jurisdictions. The level of rate determines how much revenue the property tax will generate, as the tax is generally calculated by multiplying the taxable property value with the tax rate. There are different approaches to setting property tax rates. Tax rates can be fixed in legislation or have fixed ranges that can be adjusted periodically or can be determined based on the budgetary needs. Rates can be centrally set, or locally set, or be a combination of both. In addition, tax rates can be flat versus progressive or uniform versus differentiated by property class or area. Rates can also be single or compounded.

The choice and structure of the property tax rates differ widely between the four countries. Cambodia has a flat, uniform tax rate centrally set in the legislation, which applies to all taxable properties under the law. The Philippines has ceiling rates fixed in the LGC, whereas Thailand has both ceiling rates and floor rates for the different types of properties in the Land and Building Tax. In Viet Nam, the Agricultural Land Use Tax is based on the rice price per hectare and the Non-Agricultural Land Use Tax has a mixed tax rate structure for the different uses of land. However, in general, the statutory rates are low (e.g., 0.1% in Cambodia, between 0.03% and 0.15% in Viet Nam, and capped at 0.3% in Thailand for residential properties), with the effective rates even lower.

---

[35]   Sections 3 (under b and f) and 44 of the Real Estate Services Act of the Philippines (R.A. No. 9646).

Most countries levy rates that differ by property class, such as residential, commercial, industrial, and idle land. In some countries, such as the Philippines, the rate depends on the location. Differential tax rates allow governments to manage the distribution of tax burdens across various property classes within their jurisdiction to achieve certain policy goals (e.g., promoting effective land use by putting a higher tax rate on idle land, or stimulating homeownership by taxing owner-occupied residential properties at a lower rate). Typically, agricultural and residential properties are favored, while commercial properties and vacant land, especially in the urban areas, are not. In Viet Nam, land that is not yet used under the regulation is taxed at a higher rate of 0.15% under the Non-Agricultural Land Use Tax. Thailand also places a higher ceiling rate on unutilized land, whose rate will increase with 0.3% every 3 years when left unused but capped at a total maximum 3.0%. Both Cambodia and the Philippines have a separate tax for vacant land with higher rates. In Cambodia, a 2% Tax on Unused Land is levied on unused land, including unused land with existing buildings in an abandoned state, which is a multitude of the 0.1% uniform rate set for taxable properties under the Tax on Immovable Property. In the Philippines, LGUs may collect a maximum of 5% Idle Land Tax in addition to the basic RPT, which has a ceiling rate of 1% for a province and 2% for a city or municipality within the Metropolitan Manila Area. According to Maurer and Paugam, higher taxes on vacant lots in urban areas are likely to be socially progressive and discourage speculation while fitting the fiscal objective of raising revenue (Maurer and Paugam 2000).

Some countries apply a uniform tax rate but differentiate among property classes through a classified system. In the Philippines, for example, types of property are differentiated according to ratios of assessed value but taxed at a predetermined ceiling rate of 1% or 2% depending on the location of the property. Another policy option in the tax rate structure is the choice between a uniform rate and a graduated (progressive) rate. A flat, uniform tax rate structure scores well in terms of simplicity and economic efficiency, as it tends to be neutral, but it is often perceived as regressive. A progressive tax rate structure may score well in terms of social equity, but its effects on income distribution can be difficult to measure in developing countries, where compliance and governance are weak and relevant statistics are few and sometimes inaccurate (see Chapter 3). Thailand has a progressive tax rate structure for different property categories (see Figure 5). Viet Nam also applies a progressive rate ranging between 0.03% and 0.15% for residential land depending on the area size (see Figure 6), but has a flat rate of 0.03% for residential land with multistory buildings, condominiums or underground construction works, land used for phased investment project, commercial land, and industrial land. As for agricultural land, Viet Nam uses the productive capacity of the land as a base to calculate the tax liability, which varies according to the land class category (based on land fertility, location, topography, climate condition, and irrigation) and the type of production (annual versus long term) (Loan and McCluskey 2010). For cultivated and aquacultural land, the tax rate is determined on the basis of kilograms of rice per hectare as determined in the annually published tariff schedule by the provincial people's committee. As for land used to grow wood trees and perennial trees that are harvested one time only, the tax rate is set higher at 4% of the value of the output (Shukla et al. 2011).

A simple, fairly uniform tax rate structure is generally perceived as efficient in economic terms, as different types of properties are taxed the same rate, hence limiting the risk of tax-induced distortions. Another important advantage of a uniform rate structure is that it is transparent and relatively easy to administer because the risk of tax avoidance and evasion through misclassification of properties is negligible (Norregaard 2013).

Figure 5: Tax Rate Structure of Thailand's Land and Building Tax

The ceiling and floor rates are differentiated by land and building usage (agricultural, residential, commercial and un-utilized land), within which local governments have discretion in determining the desired rated for their jurisdiction.

Agriculture
Ceiling tax rate 0.15%.

Appraised value		
Over (Baht)	Not Over (Baht)	Floor Tax Rate (%)
0	75 million	0.01
75 million	100 million	0.03
100 million	500 million	0.05
500 million	1 billion	0.07
1 billion		0.10

A tax base exemption of 50 million Baht applies to individual land and building owner. For the years 2020–2022 a transitional provision applies that exempts individual farmers completely.

Residential: Ceiling tax rate 0.30%.

For first residential home
(land and building owned by individual):

Appraised value		
Over (Baht)	Not Over (Baht)	Floor Tax Rate (%)
0	25 million	0.03
25 million	50 million	0.05
50 million		0.10

Tax base exemption of 50 million Baht for an individual land and building owner.

For other residential home:

Appraised value		
Over (Baht)	Not Over (Baht)	Floor Tax Rate (%)
0	50 million	0.02
50 million	75 million	0.03
75 million	100 million	0.05
100 million		0.10

Source: Thailand, Land and Building Tax Act B.E. 2562 (2019).

Commercial, Industrial and unutilized land
Ceiling tax rate 1.2%.

Appraised value		
Over (Baht)	Not Over (Baht)	Floor Tax Rate (%)
0	50 million	0.3
50 million	200 million	0.4
200 million	1 billion	0.5
1 billion	5 billion	0.6
5 billion		0.7

For unutilized land: the tax rate will increase 0.3% every three years for properties left unused, but will not exceed 3.0%.

For first residential home
(only building owned by individual):

Appraised value		
Over (Baht)	Not Over (Baht)	Floor Tax Rate (%)
0	40 million	0.02
45 million	65 million	0.03
65 million	90 million	0.05
90 million		0.10

Tax base exemption of 10 million Baht for an individual building owner.

Tax Rate (%)	Taxable Land Area (m²)
0.03	Area within the set quota.
	Residential land of multistory buildings with many households, condominiums or underground construction, including use for commercial purposes;
	Nonagricultural production and business land;
	Other types o non-agricultural lands that are not originally used for business purposes (such as land for cemetery, public interest, or heritage site purposes, etc.) but are later converted to business purposes
	Land of a phased investment project as registered by the investor and approved by a competent state agency
0.07	Area in excess of up to 3 times the set quota
0.15	Are in excess of over 3 times the set quota
	Land use for inappropriate purposes or land not yet used under regulations.
0.20	Encroached or appropriated land area.

Figure 6: Tax Rate Structure of Viet Nam's Non-Agricultural Land Use Tax

Source: Article 7 of the Law on Non-Agricultural Land Use Tax. Viet Nam (see Tax Rate Structure of Viet Nam's Non-Agricultural Land Use Tax).

The level of local fiscal autonomy in determining the tax rates varies widely between countries. In some countries, local authorities have the freedom to determine the rate levels and the amount of revenue they need to raise from property tax based on their expenditure requirements. In the Philippines, LGUs can determine the rate levels not exceeding the statutory ceiling rates and the assessment levels based on the amount of revenue they want to raise from property tax. In Thailand, local governments have discretionary autonomy in determining the tax rates for their jurisdiction after 2 years when the law is entered into force; however, this determination should be within the centrally set floor and ceiling rates for the various categories of property use. On the other side of the spectrum, in countries like Cambodia and Viet Nam, the rates are essentially set by the central government. A higher degree of local discretion in the rate setting often leads to greater differences in rate levels within a country.

The structure of tax rates and rate setting in the four countries are summarized in Table 6.

Property Valuation

Countries use different methods to determine the value element of taxable properties. Some countries apply an area-based assessment system, others apply a value-based system (e.g., market value or annual rental value), and sometimes a combination of both is applied. The choice of the valuation method relies on a variety of factors, including the maturity of the real estate market, the availability and access to reliable data (e.g., on ownership information, property characteristics, property sales prices), and the institutional capacity and capability to provide objective assessments of valuation. Under an area-based system, the tax liability relates directly to the size of the land and/or buildings depending on the location, quality of the structure, or other factors. Area-based assessments are often found in countries with underdeveloped property markets where market value is difficult to determine. Viet Nam's Agricultural land use tax can be considered an area-based system, as the tax is calculated on the basis of the area of land and the land categories. The latter is dependent on the nature of land, its location, climate, irrigation conditions, and average productivity obtained in normal conditions.

With the introduction of the Non-Agricultural Land Use Tax in 2012, Viet Nam made a move toward a land value-based system, albeit not based on the market value. The basis of the tax is simply the taxable land area multiplied by the price per square meters as determined by the municipal or PPC every 5 years. Depending on the municipality, the current land price schedules are estimated at 30%–70% below the actual market value. Under the draft Property Tax Law, which includes improvements on land in the tax base, Viet Nam is considering

Table 6:   Tax Rate Structure, Levels, and Rate Setting

Country	Name of Instrument	Tax Rate Structure and Levels			Tax Rate Setting	
		Flat	Differentiated	Progressive	Centrally Set	Locally Set
Cambodia	Tax on Immovable Property	0.1%			✓	
	Tax on Unused Land	2%			✓	
Philippines	Real Property Tax	Max. 1%	Province			✓
		Max. 2%	City or Municipality in Metro Manila Area			
	Idle Land Tax	Max. 5%				✓
Thailand	Land and Building Tax		Agriculture	0.01%–0.15%		✓
			Residential:			
			- *first home (land and building)*	0.03%–0.30%		
			- *first home (only building)*	0.02%–0.30%		
			- *second home*	0.02%–0.30%		
			Commercial and industrial	0.30%–1.20%		
			Un-utilized land	0.30%–3.00%		
Viet Nam	Non-agricultural Land Use Tax		Residential land	0.03%–0.15%	✓	
		0.03%	Condominium, commercial, industrial, construction			
		0.15%	Improper use or not yet used			
		0.20%	Encroached or appropriated land			
	Agricultural Land Use Tax	Rice price/ha	Land class category			✓
		4%	Timber trees, perennial crops			

ha = hectare.
Source: Authors, based on analysis of the listed legal instruments.

using a value-based approach. For newly constructed buildings, the valuation will be based on the unit price per square meters of floor size by housing grades and categories as established by the PPC in accordance with the applicable legislation on construction. For building already in use, the valuation for new construction will be adjusted with a percentage of residual useful life for buildings as determined by the PPC (Article 7 of the draft Law on Property Tax).

Market value (or capital value) assessment, commonly used in OECD countries, is based on comparable sale prices between a willing buyer and a willing seller in an arm's-length transaction. Some countries, however, do not tax the full market value as it may be incompatible with other policy objectives, such as making housing more affordable; but the real reason may be merely to appease voters. In Cambodia, properties under the Tax on Immovable Property are taxed based on 80% of the assessed market value set by the Immovable Properties Appraisal and Valuation Commission. In practice, the assessed market value is much lower than the actual market value. Similarly, in the Philippines, although properties are appraised at fair market value, the taxable value is determined by the applying assessment level to the market value of properties (see Figure 7). The assessment levels are fixed by ordinances at the local level, depending on the classification and actual use of the property and not exceeding the rates set under LGC1991 (Section 218).

Some countries assess the property according to the estimated rental value or net rent to reflect that taxes are paid from (presumptive) income rather than from wealth. Thailand's House and Land Tax, which was repealed and replaced by the Land and Buildings Tax Act (BE 2562) on 13 March 2019, was a tax based on rental income value. Under the new law, Thailand is moving toward a market value approach. The assessment base would be the total appraised value of property (including both buildings and land) as set by the Treasury Department. Buildings will be appraised using the "cost method," which is calculated as the cost price of construction, with data from the Ministry of Commerce (commercial prices) and Labor (labor costs), times the profit per square unit per province. Lands are appraised using the "market comparison method," which uses data from listed sales prices from the Department of Land. Once a price is set for an area, each parcel will be valuated according to its size.

Fair and productive property taxes require both good initial assessment and periodic reassessments (or indexing by rate of inflation, although this does not ensure accurate values as reassessment does) to reflect changes in value. The frequency with which valuations are updated varies in the four countries, even within a jurisdiction. In

Table 7:   Property Valuation System

| Country | Name of Instrument | Value-Based | | Area-Based | Frequency | Authority |
		Market Value Approach	Other			
Cambodia	Tax on Immovable Property	✓			Every 5 years	Ministry of Economy and Finance
	Tax on Unused Land	✓			Every 1 year	
Philippines	Real Property Tax	✓			Every 3 years	LGUs
	Idle Land Tax	✓				
Thailand	Land and Building Tax	✓			Every 4 years	Treasury Department
Viet Nam	Non-Agricultural Land Use Tax			✓	Every 5 years	PPC
	Agricultural Land Use Tax		✓			

LGU = local government unit, PPC = provincial people's committee.
Source: Authors, based on analysis of the listed legal instruments.

the Philippines, even though the LGC requires LGUs to reappraise every 3 years (Section 219), in practice, from the 227 total LGUs only 83 LGUs have updated the SMVs in the past 3 years. Some LGUs have not updated over 20 years due to political or administrative reasons. In some countries, the property valuation and re-evaluations are done at the central level. In Thailand, the Treasury Department is responsible for the valuation and reappraisal of all properties and plots. In Cambodia, the Immovable Properties Appraisal and Valuation Commission, led by the Ministry of Economy and Finance, assesses the property values with the input from other ministries and local stakeholders. For the Tax on Unused Land, the market value of land per square meter is determined by the Commission of Valuation of Unused Land, also under the political responsibility of the Ministry of Economy and Finance. In other countries, the valuation processes are decentralized. In Viet Nam, the PPC issues the land price schedule, which is multipurpose and valid for 5 years. In the Philippines, LGUs exercise significant control over the valuation of properties under the SMVs. To improve the quality of valuation by LGUs and to make revaluations more frequent and attuned to market developments, a bill (the Real Property Valuation and Assessment Reform Act (House Bill 4664)) is proposed that seeks to depoliticize and recentralize the approval of SMVs from the LGU to the secretary of the Department of Finance and sets the mandatory updating of the SMV every 3 years.

The choice of valuation system and the frequency of revaluation in the four countries are summarized in Table 7.

Exemption Policies and Tax Reliefs

Exemptions are commonplace and can be based on factors such as ownership (e.g., property owned and occupied by the government, international organizations, foreign embassies), the use of the property (e.g., public schools, hospitals, libraries, parks, cemeteries, and so on and property used for charitable or religious purposes), or the characteristics of the owner or occupiers (e.g., household income, age or disability, war veteran). In addition, most tax systems also provide tax relief or payment schemes to residential property owners or occupants depending on their financial position. There are sound rationales for granting exemptions and other forms of property tax relief. Exemptions for government-owned and used properties are often provided for administrative simplicity reasons, as taxing such would entail a "pay out and claw back" arrangement. Exemptions of international organizations and foreign embassies are based on international arrangements and treaty obligations. Exemptions for properties used by charitable, educational, and religious institutions can be justified based on the rationale that they offer meaningful services to society that government otherwise might have to provide. Some countries only start taxing buildings and other constructs on land when those improvements are being used. Cambodia, for example, exempts buildings of which less than 80% are still under construction and which have not been used.

Most countries have a basic exemption in their national laws to exclude low-value properties. Depending on its design—and provided that the threshold is set low enough—base exemptions are equitable as this favors income progressivity and could improve the fiscal performance of property taxes due to lower collection costs (Shukla et al. 2011). Cambodia, for example, has a general exemption of KHR100 million (approx. USD 25,000), which applies to the assessed market value of all taxable properties under the Tax on Immovable Property. In the Philippines, the base exemption applies only to building and structures (not on land) and is differentiated by types of properties: PHP175,000 (approx. USD 3,400) for residential properties and PHP300,000 (approx. USD 5,800) for buildings and structures classified as agricultural, commercial, industrial, and timberland. Some other countries apply a base exemption only to principal residential properties with the objective to cushion residents from excessive property tax burdens and to stimulate home ownership. Viet Nam is considering introducing a general exemption of VND700 million (approx. USD 30,000) for residential houses or buildings under the new property tax law. In Thailand, the base exemption is only applicable to agricultural properties and to residential properties that serve as the primary residence for the individual property owner. A base exemption of THB50 million

Figure 7: Assessment Levels in the Philippines

A. On lands:

Class	Assessment Levels (%)
Residential	20
Agricultural	40
Commercial, Industrial and Mineral	50
Timberland	20

B. On buildings and other structures:

Fair Market Value		Assessment Levels			
Over (PHP)	Not Over (PHP)	Residential (%)	Agricultural (%)	Commercial/ Industrial (%)	Timberland (%)
0	175,000.00	0			
175,000.00	300,000.00	10			
300,000.00			25	30	45
300,000.00	500,000.00	20	30	35	50
500,000.00	750,000.00	25	35	40	55
750,000.00	1,000,000.00	30	40	50	60
1,000,000.00	2,000,000.00	35	45	60	65
2,000,000.00	5,000,000.00	40	50	70	70
5,000,000.00	10,000,000.00	50	50	75	70
10,000,000.00		60	50	80	70

C. On machines:

Class	Assessment Levels (%)
Agricultural	40
Residential	50
Commercial	80
Industrial	80

D. On special classes: The assessment levels for all lands, buildings, machines, and other improvements:

Actual Use	Assessment Levels (%)
Cultural	15
Scientific	15
Hospital	15
Local water districts	10
Government-owned or controlled corporations engaged in the supply and distribution of water and/or generation and transmission of electric power	10

Source: Local Government Code 1991, Section 218.

(approx. USD 1.6 million) applies to agricultural and residential land and building, and an exemption of THB10 million (approx. USD 325,000) for residential buildings only. Second homes, unused land, and properties used for commercial and industrial purposes are fully taxed.

All countries surveyed for this report have preferential regimes in place to achieve certain land use goals, such as low rates or exemptions for farmland and forests to prevent conversion to urban development or exemptions for business property operating in certain economic zones. Cambodia, Viet Nam, and the Philippines have tax exemptions for properties that are located in special economic zones. In Thailand, the new Land and Building Tax Act provides a broad tax reduction clause of up to 90% for reasons such as economic necessity or social context to be further specified in the ministerial regulations. In the National Legislative Assembly's research report prepared before the act was drafted, tax reductions were proposed for property located in special economic zones.

All property tax systems provide some kind of tax relief to residential property owners and occupants. The intention behind such schemes is often to cushion certain residents from excessive property tax burden, to address the issue of "asset rich and cash poor," while making the property tax politically more palatable and socially acceptable. These measures can be comprehensive, such as in Cambodia, where a general exemption of KHR100 million (approx. USD 25,000) applies to the assessed market value of all properties, or selective, favoring only certain qualifying taxpayers based on factors such as age, disability, military service, household income, or property value. In Viet Nam, for example, residential property of persons who participated in the revolution prior to 19 August 1945, war invalids, war patients, war martyrs' families, and so on is exempt from property tax. In Thailand, farmers and first residential property owners benefit from a high exemption threshold.

Table 8:   Tax Exemptions, Preferential Regimes, and Tax Reliefs

Country	Tax Exemptions	Preferential Regimes	Tax Relief
Cambodia	Agricultural; government; religion, charity; embassy/consulate; international organizations; public infrastructure; force majeure; buildings of which less than 80% still under construction	Economic zones	Base exemption of KHR100 million for all taxable properties
Philippines	Government; charity, religion, education; nonprofit cemeteries; machineries/equipment for water supply, electricity power and transmission, and environmental protection; property owned by registered cooperatives	Economic zones. RPT might be included in the list of exempt taxes under the proposed tax amnesty bill	Base exemption for buildings/structures (PHP175,000 for residential; PHP300,000 for agricultural, commercial, industrial and timberland)
Thailand	Government, state enterprises; international organizations, embassy/consulate; Thai Red Cross Society; religion; nonprofit public cemetery/crematorium; charity; public use, public utility	Maximum 90% reductions for economic or social context	Base exemption of TBH50 million for agricultural and residential land and buildings; TBH10 million for residential buildings
Viet Nam	Agricultural land serving research, experimental production, annual crops, salt production; state or state-owned farms and plantations; establishments for education, healthcare, cultural, sports, or environmental activities; care facilities for pensioners, disabled and orphans; land in disadvantaged areas; historical-cultural sites	Economic zones; investment project in areas with socioeconomic difficulties; enterprises employing war invalids and diseased soldiers	War invalids, diseased soldiers, armed forces heroes, heroic Vietnamese mothers, martyrs, Agent Orange victims, poor households, taxpayers suffering from natural disasters or other hardships

RPT = real property tax.
Source: Authors, based on analysis of the legal instruments.

Summary

From a bird's eye view, the property tax system of the four countries share some common basic design features: an annual tax on ownership or occupation of immovable property, payable by the owner and/or occupant, calculated by multiplying the taxable property value—typically based on some form of market value approach—with a tax rate, which is often higher for unused or vacant land; a wide range of tax exemptions that generally include state-owned properties, historic and cultural sites, agricultural land, and properties used by nonprofit and international organizations; and tax reliefs to vulnerable taxpayers. However, viewed closely, the property taxes are diverse, complex, and constantly under review for further improvement.

One of the most striking differences between the four property tax systems is the tax base, which is generally narrow. While Viet Nam taxes land only (site value taxation), with land directly used for agricultural productions being tax exempt, the coverage of Cambodia's Tax on Immovable Property is limited to land and improvements located in the urban areas. In Thailand, most owner-occupied residences are exempt from tax due to the generous base exemption per the Land and Building tax. The tax serves as an actual recurrent tax on immovable property for high-net-worth individuals who own a primary residential home (land and building) with an appraised value of more than THB50 million in Thailand and for those who own a residential condominium or an apartment unit worth over THB10 million and for second home owners. Of the four countries, the Philippines has the broadest tax base, which includes not only land and building, but also machinery and other permanent or temporary additions or improvements on, above, and below ground, including natural resources in their original state.

As shown in Table 6, the tax rate structure and levels, as well as the degree of local discretion in the rate setting, differ widely between the countries. Cambodia has a centrally set flat rate of 0.1% that is uniformly applicable to all taxable properties under the Tax on Immovable Property and a higher rate of 2% for unused land. Thailand has a progressive tax rate structure for different property categories with centrally set ceiling and floor rates, within which local governments have discretion in determining the desired rate levels for their jurisdiction. In the Philippines, LGUs also have the powers to set a uniform rate not exceeding the statutory ceiling rates of 1% for properties located in a province and 2% for properties located in a city or a municipality within the Metropolitan Manila Area. Although the Philippines applies a uniform tax rate, properties are differentiated by class and actual use through the assessment levels, which are flat for lands, machines, and special use, and progressive for buildings and other structures (see Figure 8). Viet Nam has also a mixed rate structure: progressive rates for residential land and flat rates for different land class categories and usage.

In terms of valuation, most countries apply a value-based system to determine the value element of their taxable properties. Thailand has recently moved away from an annual rental income value toward a market value approach. Cambodia and the Philippines also assess properties according to the market value, but the tax is calculated at a lower, adjusted value. In Cambodia, properties under the Tax on Immovable Property are taxed based on 80% of the assessed market value. Similarly, in the Philippines, the taxable value is determined by applying assessment levels to the market value of properties, which are fixed by ordinances at the local level, depending on the classification and actual use of the property and not exceeding the rates set under LGC 1991 (Section 218). Viet Nam, by contrast, has an area-based system, but is considering adopting a value-based approach under the new property tax regime.

V. Property Registration and Fiscal Cadastre

Introduction

Among the principal prerequisites for effective property taxation are adequate systems of property registration and fiscal cadastre, implanted within the context of a country-specific socioeconomic, institutional, political, and administrative situation. As emphasized in the UN-HABITAT policy guide on land and property tax,[36] when implementing a property tax system, the policy and administrative choices should be informed by knowledge of the following four considerations:

- the system should take into account the accepted institutions and traditions related to land and property rights;

- the supporting fiscal cadastre system must reflect the realities of the current formal and informal systems for registering and acknowledging property rights;

- the property tax system should also attend carefully to market conditions in different locations and for different types of property; and

- when designing the property tax system, the administrative capacity and processes for implementing the system must be carefully considered.

This chapter focuses on the registration of land and property rights and the fiscal cadastre systems in the four benchmarking countries.

What Are Land and Property Rights?

How a country regards land and property rights may shape the policy choices in the property tax system related to the tax subject (who should pay the tax), the range of tax exemptions, and the administrative measures on how to collect and enforce the tax. According to the related literature, two views can be discerned regarding land and property rights: one that argues that land and identity are closely tied together and considers property to be a human right, and the other that sees land as an economic commodity separate from the sense of identity (Joireman and Brown 2013). Countries that are more inclined to the former view, which is the case in all four countries in this study, might have a strong social justice component in their constitution that recognizes the rights of, for example, farmers and indigenous people to lands while restricting foreign ownership. In such a setting, the social justice component is often reflected in the policy choices regarding tax rate differentials or exemption policies in the

---

36   UN-HABITAT. 2011. *Land and Property Tax: A Policy Guide.* Nairobi: United Nations Human Settlements Programme.

property tax system. Countries that subscribe more to the latter view might rely stronger on the mechanisms of free market economy where property rights can be easily traded and mortgaged for the gain of financial capital. Subsequently, the policy choices supporting this view would place a higher emphasis on simplicity and neutrality, with limited exemptions and rate differentials that may distort economic behavior. How a country perceives land and property rights changes over time and may be influenced by factors such as urbanization, natural disasters, and conflicts.

Another important distinction that can be made regarding to land and property rights is whether or not private ownership is accepted. If individual private ownership is accepted, the incidence of the property tax should fall on land and property owners, and failure to pay the tax could invoke the government's right to seize and sell the land to recover the unpaid taxes. In contrast, countries that do not recognize private land ownership rights, the incidence of the property tax should fall on the occupant or user of lands and tax administrators would need to be able to secure tax payments against other assets than the land if the taxpayer fails to pay the tax (Joireman and Brown 2013). Viet Nam, for example, does not recognize private ownership of land, as land is considered "public property, owned by all the people, and represented and uniformly managed by the State" under its Constitution (art. 53). The state, however, may grant land use rights to individuals, households, and organizations for different periods of time in accordance with the provisions of the Land Law.[37] Land users (both domestic and foreign) have many rights, which are recognized and protected by the state under the law, including the right to enjoy the results of labor and investment on land, but also the right to exchange, transfer, lease, sublease, donate, and mortgage land use rights.[38] Although Viet Nam does not recognize private land ownership, private home ownership, on the other hand, is allowed. Under the Housing Law, domestic organizations, households, and individuals, overseas Vietnamese, as well as foreign organizations and individuals are entitled to own houses in Viet Nam.[39] With respect to foreign house ownership, only qualifying foreign investors and individuals permitted to enter Viet Nam may own houses in Viet Nam within a set quota (which is limited to 30% of the number of apartments in a condominium or 250 houses, including villas and semidetached houses, in an area with a population equivalent to a ward-level administrative unit) and duration (foreign individuals may only own houses for a maximum of 50 years from the date they are granted the certificate and may enjoy extensions under government regulations. Foreign organizations may own houses within the term stated in their investment certificates, including also extended duration).[40] A foreign individual who is married to a Vietnamese citizen or an overseas Vietnamese has the same homeownership rights as Vietnamese citizens (freehold).

Cambodia, the Philippines, and Thailand recognize private ownership for both land and buildings; however, private ownership of land is in principle restricted to citizens, while private ownership of buildings and other structures is allowed for foreigners under certain conditions. Under the Cambodian Constitution, only a natural person or legal entity of Khmer nationality shall have the right to land ownership. A legal entity is considered to be Cambodian when at least 51% of its shares are owned by Cambodian citizen(s) or by Cambodian legal entities. Foreigners may own up to 70% of co-owned buildings, provided that they do not own any real property on the ground floor and underground. Likewise in the Philippines, only Filipino citizens and legal entities, that is, corporations or associations with at least 60% of the capital owned by Philippines' citizen, are entitled to own or acquire land.[41] Under the Condominium Act (R.A. 4726), foreigners may purchase no more than 40% of the units of a condominium project or shares in condominium corporations. In addition, foreign individuals or corporations may enter into a lease

---

[37]   See Article 4 of Viet Nam's Land Law 2013 (No. 45/2013/QH13): "Land belongs to the entire-people and the State acts as the representative of the land ownership and uniformly manages land. The State grants land use rights to the land users in accordance with the provisions of this Law."

[38]   See Chapter 11 Rights and Obligations of Land Users of the Land Law 2013 (No. 45/2013/QH13).

[39]   See Article 7 of the Housing Law 2014 (No. 65/2014/QH13).

[40]   Article 161 of the Housing Law 2014.

[41]   Though exemptions apply to acquisitions before the 1935 Constitution, cases of hereditary succession and purchase by former natural-born Filipino citizen under certain restrictions.

agreement with Filipino owners for an initial period up to 50 years and renewable for an additional 25 years under the Investor's Lease Act (R.A. 7652). In Thailand, land ownership is also restricted to Thai citizens and legal entities (i.e., at least 51% of the capital is owned by a Thai citizen or more than half of the total number of shareholders are Thai citizens). To stimulate foreign direct investment, an exemption is made for qualifying foreign investors who bring in capital for investment of more than THB40 million (approx. USD 1.25 million) in projects that are deemed economically and socially beneficial to Thailand. Under this investment promotion scheme, foreigners may acquire no more than 1 *rai* (or 1,600 m²) of land within the locality of Bangkok Metropolitan Administration, the City of Pattaya, a municipality, or the zone designated to be the residential area under the law on city planning. As of January 2019, only 8 foreign investors have purchased land via this investment promotion scheme (based on data from the Department of Land). With regard to foreign ownership of condominiums, qualifying foreign investors may own up to 49% of the total space of apartments at the time of applying for registration of condominium. For ownership of condominium units located in Bangkok Metropolis, municipalities or other local administrative areas as prescribed in the ministerial regulations, a foreign ownership ratio higher than 49% is allowed; however, the land area where the condominium is located plus the land area provided for joint use benefits of joint owners must not exceed 5 *rais* (8,000 m²).

Table 9:   Rights to Land and Property

| Country | Land Rights | | Property Rights | |
	Private Ownership	Private Foreign Ownership	Private Ownership	Private Foreign Ownership
Cambodia	Yes, restricted to Cambodian citizens and legal entities	No, unless through legal entity with less than 49% foreign-owned shares	Yes	Restricted: foreigners are allowed ownership of up to 70% of co-owned buildings, provided that they do not own any real property on the ground floor and underground floor
Philippines	Yes, restricted to Filipino citizens and legal entities	No, unless: property acquired before the 1935 Constitution; acquired through hereditary succession; purchased by former natural-born Filipino citizen under certain restrictions	Yes	Restricted: foreigners may own up to 40% of condominium units and buildings, but not the land where the structures are built on A foreign individual or corporation may enter into a 50-year lease agreement with Filipino owners (renewable once for an additional 25 years)
Thailand	Yes, restricted to Thai citizens and legal entities	No, unless qualifying foreign investors	Yes	Restricted to qualifying foreign investors with condominiums not exceeding foreign ownership ratio of 49%, unless located in Bangkok Metropolis, municipalities or other local administrative areas
Viet Nam	No, land ownership rights are collective	No, land ownership rights are collective	Yes	Restricted: eligible foreign organizations, individuals and invested may own buildings within a set quota and duration Freehold for foreign spouse of Vietnamese citizen

Source: Authors, based on analysis of the Constitution and legislation in the four countries.

Land Registration System and Cadastre

Land administration generally refers to the processes of recording and disseminating information about the ownership, value, and use of land and its associated resources.[42] It is the way in which the rules of land tenure are applied and made operational through an extensive range of formal or informal systems and processes to administer land rights, land use rights, land valuation, taxation, and so on. A good land administration system can provide the following:

- Guarantee security of land tenure and property rights. Security in land tenure and property rights can spur economic growth as it encourages investment in land, increases access to formal credit, creates a more efficient land and labor market, and attracts foreign direct investment (Roth and McCarthy 2013).

- Enhance the revenue performance of property taxes. Good land records will improve efficiency and effectiveness in collecting property taxes and provide better estimates of the market value of properties.

- Reduce land disputes.

- Improve efficient land-use, facilitate rural land reform, and improve urban planning and infrastructure development.

- Support environmental and disaster management.

- Produce statistical data to support decision-making (Footnote 42).

The establishment of a cadastre is arguably the most important success factor for the development of an effective land information system (Williamson 1985). Under the term cadastre is generally understood as a parcel-based and up-to-date land information system containing a record of interest in land; it includes a geometric description of land parcels linked to other records or registers describing the nature of the interests, and ownership or control of those interests, and often the value to the parcel and its improvements.[43] Cadastral systems usually comprise a land registration system and a cadastral survey and/or mapping system as key components (Williamson 1997).

Registration of Deed versus Registration of Title

There are two broad categories of land registration: the registration of deed and the registration of title. The former is concerned with the registration of the legal instrument describing the transfer of rights (chain of deeds), while the latter is concerned with the registration of the right (i.e., title) itself (Henssen 1995). A registration of deed provides evidence that a particular transaction has taken place and protects the property owner with the registered deed from claims based on an unregistered one. However, the deed in itself does not prove title nor the validity of the legal rights of the parties carrying out the transaction (Zevenbergen 2002). The registry is simply a place of records of legal facts and documents. Deeds registration is common in Europe (France, Spain, Italy, Belgium, Luxemburg, and the Netherlands), in South America, most of the United States, and parts of Asia and Africa. In contrast, title registration is intended to reflect the correct legal situation (Henssen 1995, Zevenbergen 2002). Under a title registration, the act of registration confers legal status and serves as proof of property ownership, and as a consequence, greater responsibility is placed upon the state to analyze the validity of documents to avoid damages and compensation. Germany, Austria, Switzerland, the Nordic countries, and parts of Eastern Europe have a system of title registration. The four countries in this study also have a title registration, though some differences exist.

[42]   ECE. 1996. *Land Administration Guidelines.* No. ECE/HBP/96. Geneva: Economic Commission for Europe /United Nations.
[43]   The International Federation of Surveyors. 1995. FIG Statement on the Cadastre. *FIG Publication.* No. 11.

In Cambodia, the act of registration of "hard titles" confers legal status on the rights in real property. When a new property owner is registered in the system, the cadastral office issues a public display of data of land parcels, against which interested parties may object. If no objections are received within a given period (15 days of public display), the ownership is definite. In cases of omissions or disputes, interested parties can seek rectification at the cadastral office or lodge an appeal first at the three level of cadastral committee and subsequently at the court to verify the historical ownership of the property. The government, however, does not have a system to compensate for loss suffered by an omission or error in the cadastre.

Likewise, in Viet Nam, the act of registration equates to the declaration and acknowledgement of the legal status of land use rights, ownership of houses and other land-attached assets, and the land management right over a certain land parcel, in the cadastral records (Article 3(15) of the Land Law 2013). The registered property rights are guaranteed by the state; however, in cases of omission or errors in the registry, land users are not entitled to compensation under the Land Law (only in the event of recovery of land for national defense or security purpose or for socioeconomic development for the national or public interest according to Article 26(3) of the Land Law 2013). In the event of a dispute over the rights and obligations of land users among two or more parties in a land relationship, or disputes related to the boundaries, the state shall encourage self-reconciliation among the disputing parties. If that fails, parties may send a petition to the commune-level People's Committee of the Locality where the disputed land is located. If that fails, the dispute shall be settled by either the People's Committee or the People's Court (Articles 202–203 of the Land Law 2013).

In Thailand, the act of registration confers legal status, and registered property rights are guaranteed by the state. The land officers under the Department of Lands have extensive powers to examine, investigate, interrogate, and summon witnesses when registering any rights and juristic acts relating to land and immovable property under the Land Code. When the land officer makes a civil mistake, he is personally liable; the Land Office will pay the damage but will collect it back from the officer.

The Philippines title registry system is based on the Torrens system. The Torrens system is a system of land registration adopted in Australia by Sir Robert Torrens, which can be described as a *"registration of transactions with interests in lands whose declared object is, under governmental authority to establish and certify to the ownership of an absolute and indefeasible title to realty and to simplify its transfer. An important feature of the system is an indemnity fund to compensate any one who may be injured by the operation of the Act"* (Scott 1914, citing Hogg). Under the Philippines' system, the act of registration is not a mode of acquiring ownership, but merely a procedure to establish evidence of title over property. The competent authority for land registration (Register of Deeds) and cadastral registration (Director of Lands) has no power or jurisdiction to decide cases involving land ownership; that power is reserved to the courts. Every decree of registration issued by the Commissioner of Land Registration, however, shall bind the land, quiet title, and be conclusive against all persons, including the government. Any bona fide persons who sustain loss or damage from errors in the certificate of title or registry, may file a claim against the Register of Deeds and the National Treasurer in any court and seek compensation from the Assurance Fund.

Juridical versus Fiscal

The primary function of a cadastral system varies among countries and is usually a product of the jurisdiction's historical development, its laws, and traditional land tenure arrangements, but also its land policy priorities and method of introduction of land registration. In most countries, the cadastre is either established for juridical purposes (i.e., to serve as a legally recognized record of land tenure) or for fiscal purposes (i.e., developed for property valuation and supporting taxation on land). Modern cadastres are multipurpose and encompass both juridical and fiscal objectives with the addition of other parcel-related information.

Table 10:   Land Registration System

Country	Registration System	Missions	Registration Method	Establishment Approach
Cambodia	Registration of Title	Juridical	Compulsory	Systematic (from 2018 onward)
Philippines	Registration of Title (Torrens System)	Juridical	Optional	Sporadic and systematic
Thailand	Registration of Title	Primary: Juridical Secondary: Fiscal	Compulsory	Sporadic and systematic
Viet Nam	Registration of Title (LUR Certificates)	Primary: Juridical Secondary: Fiscal	Compulsory and optional	Sporadic and systematic

Source: Authors' analysis based on data gathered from the four countries during the Workshop on Property Registration and Fiscal Cadastre, 9–10 May 2019, Manila.

Compulsory versus Optional

The requirement for registration of land ownership can be compulsory or optional. Under a compulsory land registration, the law specifies the circumstances under which properties or property rights must be registered (e.g., transfer, partitions, consolidations, mortgages, and liens). Failure to do so would often result in a penalty. Cambodia, Thailand, and Viet Nam have a compulsory land registration. For the ownership of houses and other land-attached assets, the registration is voluntary in Viet Nam. Under a voluntary or optional registration, properties are only registered at the request and discretion of the property owner. In the Philippines, the registration of land and property rights is optional under the Property Registration Decree (P.D. 1529).

Systematic versus Sporadic

The approach for establishing cadastral records can be systematic, sporadic, or both. Under a systematic approach, all land within a designated area is brought onto the land register in a methodical and orderly sequence. In contrast, under a sporadic approach, titles are brought onto the register on a case-to-case basis, usually when a transaction occurs. Most countries have both a systematic and sporadic mechanism to land registration. In this respect it is worth mentioning that Cambodia has moved away from sporadic land registration toward a systematic one since 2018.

Institutional Framework and Oversight

The functions and responsibilities for the maintenance of the land registry and fiscal cadastre, as well as the titling, valuation, surveying, and mapping of properties, are often assigned to different tiers of government and organizations.

Cambodia

In Cambodia, the system of land registry and titling is created under the 2001 Land Law. The land registry is kept and maintained in three levels: national, provincial, and district. At the central level, the General Department of Cadastre and Geography, which falls under the MLMUPC, is responsible for registering and administering lands, conducting geodetic and cadastral surveys, and mapping and valuing properties. At the subnational level, the 165 district offices and 24 provincial and municipal offices of the MLMUPC are responsible for carrying out the actual implementation of land registration, administration of land transactions, and land use planning (i.e., to ensure that land parcels are surveyed and adjudicated in the field and that the associated ownership information is properly registered in the system).

Cambodia's cadastral system is managed by the district offices of the MLMUPC and comprises of the following components: (i) a textual component, detailing information on ownership, land parcel size, registered encumbrances, and historic data on each parcel number, and (ii) a spatial component, that is, cadastral index maps which show all land parcels graphically corresponding to the registered parcel with unique identifier in the areas where systematic land registration is implemented.[44]

There are currently two forms of land titles in Cambodia that secure property ownership: "hard title" and "soft title." Hard titles are ownership certificates issued by the General Department of Cadastre and Geography, generally under the process of systematic land registration[45] and using modern technology tools for measurement such as total station (Theodolite), electronic distance measure, global positioning system, or orthophotograph. The data are computerized to produce a cadastral index map with a uniform scale of land parcels and a correct geometry (Hem 2019). Hard title offers the strongest possessory rights status, is definitive and uncontested, and contains detailed information that has been duly recognized and certified by the central government, as well as at the *sangkat* and district level. When a hard title is being transferred, the buyer must obtain a copy of the original title certificate from the seller to verify that the seller is indeed the rightful owner and have said certificate authenticated by the district land office of the MLMUPC to ensure that there are no liens, mortgages or other encumbrances registered for that property, including any outstanding taxes on the property, such as the immovable property tax and unused land tax. In addition, a 4% transfer tax will be applied to the transfer. The 2001 Land Law prohibits transfer unless all taxes are paid. Both the seller and the buyer must apply for registration at the district office to have the name of the new owner officially inserted on the title certificate. After all taxes are paid at the Tax Collection Office, the parties may return to the Cadastral office at the MLMUPC to sign and thumb print a form of buying or selling real property, witnessed by a local authority such as a commune chief. The district land office will then forward all the transfer documents to the municipal land office where it issues the final certificate of title in the new owner's name.

The Ministry of Interior (MOI) is responsible for the certification and issuing of soft titles by local authorities. Soft titles are issued by sporadic land registration and are the most common form of ownership in Cambodia. Soft titles are considered as proof of land tenure, although they do not provide a definite title, nor are they registered at the central level or linked with the hard title registry of the MLMUPC. However, in practice, they can be used as collateral security and can be exchanged for a hard title. Soft title documentation may have different forms, such as a letter of transfer from the previous owner, a procession status certificate or a building application certified by the local authorities under the political responsibility of the MOI. When a soft title is being transferred, the new owner is only obliged to pay 4% transfer tax on the last transfer; prior unpaid transfer taxes are waived (but not the recurrent property taxes, which remain a lien on the property). In practice, tax authorities may have difficulties in collecting tax on soft titles as local authorities do not always submit the transfer documentation to the tax administration.

In terms of institutional oversight, both the MLMUPC and MOI have an internal audit and inspection department within the ministry. The National Audit Agency, a body operating under the Ministry of Economy and Finance, but reporting to the National Assembly and Senate, is responsible for supervising the registration of property

---

[44]   Centre for Spatial Data Infrastructures and Land Administration. 2019. Cadastral Template 2.0, Cambodia. http://cadastraltemplate.org/cambodia. php (accessed on 19 August 2019).

[45]   Hard titles can also be issued under sporadic land registration, provided that the process of registration also uses modern technology tools.

(internal audit). The Ministry of National Assembly Senate Relation and Inspection is an independent agency that supervises all ministries and agencies.

Philippines

In the Philippines, property registration is governed by Act 496 (The Land Registration Act, 1902), which was replaced by PD 1529 (Property Registration Decree, 1978). The titling and registration of property is based on the Torrens system. Under this system, the Land Registration Authority of the Department of Justice serves as the central repository of all land records relating to registered or titled lands. The registration of deeds and instruments pertaining to real and personal properties is carried out by the different Registries of Deeds established in each province and city throughout the country.

There are different government agencies involved in surveying and mapping activities in the Philippines. The Department of Environment and Natural Resources (DENR) is the executive department responsible for the conservation, management, protection, and sustainable development of the Philippines' environment and natural resources. Through the Land Management Bureau (LMB) and DENR regional offices, the DENR administers, surveys, and manages alienable and disposable lands and other government lands that are not placed under the jurisdiction of other government agencies. The National Mapping and Resource Information Authority, also an agency under DENR, acts as the central mapping agency, depository, and distribution facility that provides the public data on natural resources in the form of maps, charts, texts, and statistics. These activities are carried out by the five branches within the agency: the Hydrography Branch, the Mapping and Geodesy Branch, the Resource Data Analysis Branch, the Geospatial Information System Management Branch, and the Support Services Branch.[46]

The property registration information recorded by the Land Registration Authority (under the Department of Justice) and the cadastral mapping by the LMB (under DENR) are kept in different databases, which are not linked, and. separate and distinct identification numbers are used by the different registration and mapping agencies. For the registration of properties, the Registries of Deeds assigns a number on the original certificate title in case of unregistered land or issues a transfer certificate of title for registered properties, which shows the number of the next previous certificate as well as the number of the original certificate of title for that property. For the cadastral mapping, the director of Lands assigns "cadastral lot numbers" to parcels that have been filed for original proceedings. In addition, the LGC 1991 requires the establishment of a real property identification system for RPT purposes, in which all declarations of real property made under the law shall be kept and filed under a uniform classification system and managed by the provincial, city or municipal assessors.

Thailand

In Thailand, the system of immovable property registration and cadastral mapping is operated by the Department of Lands (DOL) and its land offices at the provincial, branch and district levels, under the political responsibility of the Ministry of Interior (MOI). Under section 1299 of the Commercial and Civil Code, Book IV Property, the acquisition of immovable property or property rights is not complete unless it is made in writing and is registered by the competent official, that is, the land officers in the provincial land office or the branch land office where the property is situated. The DOL is responsible for the cadastral map sheet, which is attached to the title deed of registered parcels and contains the name and address of the land rights holder, the location and area of land, as well as a map specifying the plot boundaries.

---

[46] Centre for Spatial Data Infrastructures and Land Administration. 2019. Cadastral Template 2.0, Philippines. http://cadastraltemplate.org/cadastraltemplate/philippines.php (accessed on 19 August 2019).

The cadastral system of Thailand is a parcel-based and up-to-date land information system, which consists of (i) the record of ownership (land books and condominiums registers), which includes the area and historical data of all land parcels and information on ownership, mortgages, and other encumbrances—this record is fully computerized and managed by the Land Registry Standard Bureau; and (ii) cadastral maps, survey documentation, and geodetic information files relating to the registered title with unique identifiers, managed by the Survey Standard and Promotion Bureau.[47] The information is recorded in a central, integrated database at the DOL. Data kept and maintained at the local land offices are linked to the central DOL database.

In terms of oversight, the chief of Land Office is authorized to supervise the operation of property registration. In addition, the Audit Department and the inspectors in the Department of Lands, operating under the Ministry of Interior, may conduct audits.

Viet Nam

In Viet Nam, the 2013 Land Law stipulates that a comprehensive, multipurpose land information system, including a national land database, shall be uniformly developed nationwide (Art. 120 Land Law). The latter includes databases for legal documentation on lands, cadastral records, land statistics and inventories, master plans and plans on land use, land prices, land investigations, dispute settlements, and other land-related records (Art. 121 Land Law). The Ministry of Natural Resources and Environment (MONRE) is primarily responsible for developing and managing the aforementioned land information system and national land database, and for providing electronic public services relating to land. Other ministries and government agencies are required by law to provide all land-related information and data to MONRE to update the national land database and land information system. At the local level, the PPC organizes the development, management, and exploitation of the land information system and the land databases in their localities and subsequently provides land data to MONRE to integrate into the central systems.

Under MONRE, the following state administrative offices (which are consultative units to assist the minister in carrying out public administrative functions) are in charge of land administration: (i) the General Department of Land Administration, (ii) the Department of Survey and Mapping, and (iii) the Department of Information Technology. MONRE also has state enterprises that supply services in the fields of cadastre, meteorology, geodesy, and cartography.

Under the government's decree,[48] the responsibility for the (i) registration of land and other land-attached assets, (ii) collection and management of cadastral records and land databases, (iii) preparation of land statistics and inventory, and (iv) exchange of land information upon request to interested parties under regulations, is delegated to the land registration offices. These offices are public service units of provincial-level Departments of Natural Resources and Environment and have branches in districts, towns, and provincial cities. The Department of Natural Resources and Environment is responsible for granting certificates of land use rights and ownership of houses and other related land-attached assets to land users and owners of land-attached assets.

---

[47]   Centre for Spatial Data Infrastructures and Land Administration. 2019. Cadastral Template 2.0, Thailand. http://cadastraltemplate.org/thailand. php (accessed on 19 August 2019).

[48]   Decree detailing a number of articles of the Land Law, No. 43/2014/ND-CP dated 15 May 2014, as amended and supplemented by Decree No. 01/2017/ND-CP dated 6 January 2017.

Table 11:   Institutional Framework

Country	Ministry	Agency (National or Local Level)	Functions
Cambodia	Ministry of Land Management, Urban Planning and Construction (MLMUPC)	*National level:* General Department of Cadastre and Geography (GDCG)	Systematic land registration; land administration; geodetic and cadastral surveying, mapping; property valuation; certification and issuing of hard titles
		Local level: 24 provincial/municipal offices and 165 district offices of MLMUPC	Implementation of land registration; administration of land transactions; land use planning; surveying and field investigation; recording land ownership in the land registry; certification and issuing of hard titles
	Ministry of Interior (MOI)	*Local level:* Local authorities	Certification and issuing of soft titles
Philippines	Department of Justice (DOJ)	*National level:* Land Registration Authority (LRA)	Central repository of records; issuing decrees of registration, registration of land transactions
		Local level: Registries of Deeds	Competent authority for registration of deeds; issuing original certificate title (OCT) and transfer certificates of title (TCT)
	Department of Environment and Natural Resources (DENR)	*National level:* Land Management Bureau (LMB)/DENR regional offices	Verifying and approving original survey plans; conducting cadastral survey; land administration and land management; issuing cadastral lot numbers
		Local level: Natural Mapping and Resource Information Authority (NAMRIA): - Mapping and Geodesy Branch (MGB) - Geospatial Information System Management Branch (GISMB)	Cadastral mapping, central depository of maps, charts text and statistics on land
Thailand	Ministry of Interior (MOI)	*National level:* Department of Lands: - Land Registry Standard Bureau - Survey Standard and Promotion Bureau - Information Technology Bureau - Mapping Technology Bureau - Land Document Issuance Standard Bureau	Responsible for the management of land information system, land survey and mapping, issuance of land title deeds, registration of property and property transactions, cadastral map sheets
		Local level: - Provincial Land Offices - Branch Land Offices - District Land Offices	Competent authority for registration of immovable properties, property rights and juristic acts; management and maintenance of land parcel maps and land ownership

Table 11:   Institutional Framework *(continued)*

Country	Ministry	Agency (National or Local Level)	Functions
Viet Nam	Ministry of Natural Resources and Environment (MONRE)	*National level:* General Department of Land Administration (GDLA)	Responsible for cadastral system including land register, cadastral mapping, cadastral documentation, land tenure certificate issuance, and land record system update; Land investigation and inventory of land classification, land assessment, and land valuation
			Land statistics and current land use mapping; Compensation for recovery of land
		Local level: - Provincial-level Natural Resources and Environment Departments (DONRE)	Granting certificates of land use rights (LUR) and ownership of houses and other related land-attached assets to land users and owners of land-attached assets
		- District-level People's Committees	LRO is responsible for:
		Land Registration Offices (LRO)	(i) registering land and other land-attached assets; (ii) collecting, managing, updating and uniformly revising cadastral dossier and land databases; (iii) preparing land statistics and inventory; and (iv) disseminating land information to the public

Source: Authors' analysis based on data gathered from the four countries during the Workshop on Property Registration and Fiscal Cadastre, 9–10 May 2019, Manila.

Fiscal Cadastre

Implementing an effective property tax system would require the development of a fiscal cadastre, which records information about taxpayers, properties with parcel boundaries and building information, land use, valuations, and assessments for tax purposes. This can be distinguished from a legal cadastre, which lists title or ownership to land and buildings for legal purposes. The functions of juridical and fiscal land recording, surveying, and mapping can either be integrated in one organization (such as the case in Viet Nam) or performed under different organizations where the information needed for tax purposes has been coordinated into one information system or arranged in such a way that different systems can exchange information. A common concern raised among the four countries is the lack of coordination between government organizations on the systematic exchange of records and/or the lack of data compatibility between the different information systems. An important challenge some countries face is that government organizations work in silos. The development of modern land information system using computer technology has been a catalyst for closer coordination among organizations.

A fiscal cadastre is usually layered or built upon the legal cadastre; however, this is not the case in Cambodia. A separate, stand-alone database with records on taxpayers, properties, and payment history was created on the basis of taxpayers' self-assessment forms (the PT01 tax form) and is kept and maintained at the local tax branches of the General Department of Taxation (GDT) for the purpose of the immovable property tax and unused land tax. Data derived from the PT01 tax form include the property owner's information (number of owners, the names, addresses, and tax identification numbers), and information on the property itself (address, size, building type, and year of construction). In addition, the Property Survey Working Group of the GDT conducts surveys to update all relevant property information in the tax database, which allows the Property Tax Office (GDT) to verify the self-declared information by taxpayers and to ensure that property owners register and declare their properties at the tax office. When a transfer of hard title occurs, the district land office submits transfer documentation to the tax office for the collection of taxes. However, in the event of soft titles, tax authorities do not always receive such documentation from the local authorities. The GDT is currently in the process of improving data exchange with MLMUPC. In addition, the government is conducting a study to adopt legislation that will provide the tax administration full powers to obtain information and data from relevant government institutions for tax purposes.

In the Philippines, all relevant data for purposes of real property taxation are being kept and maintained by the provincial, city or municipal assessors at the LGU level across the nation under a uniform classification system. Pursuant to the LGC 1991, the registrar of deeds, the buildings officials, and geodetic engineers (public or private) are, respectively, mandated to submit periodically to the assessors:

- an abstract of the registry which contains descriptions of the registered real properties, current ownership information, dates of latest transfer or alienation accompanied by copies of the corresponding deeds of sale, donation or other forms of alienation;

- a copy of building permit for the construction, addition, repair or renovation of a building or a permanent improvement on land, and certificate of registration of machinery, including machines, mechanical contrivances and apparatus attached or affixed on land or to another real property within 30 days of issuance; and

- a copy of all approved original or subdivision plans or maps of surveys from the LMB, the land Registration Authority, and the Housing and Land Use Regulatory Board.

With the technical assistance provided under the ADB Domestic Resource Mobilization Trust Fund,[49] the Philippines is currently in the process of developing an interlinked information technology system with the different government agencies, which will allow the LGUs to gain direct access to property-related databases and registries for tax purposes.

In Thailand, there are three agencies involved in the fiscal cadastre development and maintenance: the Department of Land (cadastre), Treasury Department (property valuation or appraisal) and the Department of Local Government Administration (taxation mapping). With the introduction of the new Land and Buildings Tax, which came into effect on 1 January 2020, the government is developing a new centralized property tax database to merge the data from the three departments. The data from the Department of Lands (cadastre) will be enhanced with property values from the Treasury and provided in a template for some 7,700 local government offices to add their local tax information.

In Viet Nam, all land-related information, including the valuation of property, are kept and maintained in a central government database under MONRE. For the assessment and collection of the property taxes, the system relies on self-assessment and payment by land users at the local tax offices.

Person-Based vs. Property-Based

Fiscal cadastre can either be person (taxpayer)-based or property (map)-based. A person-based cadastre lists the persons, both physical and legal, and information about the properties they are known to possess (Fung and McAuley 2020). Such cadastre is dependent on the owners to submit accurate declarations of their land and buildings holdings. Both Cambodia and Viet Nam have a person-based cadastre. In contrast, a property-based cadastre is organized by property, which holds information on the location but also the owners and/or users.

---

[49] ADB Domestic Resource Mobilization TF project on "National Property Tax and IT Valuation Reform Implementation."

Property-based cadastres make it possible to verify whether all land and buildings have been accounted for and registered (Almy and Cusack 2017). The Philippines has a property-based cadastre, while Thailand has moved from a person-based to a property-based system with the recent reform.

Table 12:   Fiscal Cadastre

Country	Registration System	Ministry	Agency (National or Local Level)	Functions
Cambodia	Person-based	Ministry of Economy and Finance	General Department of Taxation (GDT)	Property registration and tax information system
			Local tax branch	(i) Registration of immovable properties and updates (e.g., change in size, demolition, ownership) via tax form PT01
				(ii) Issuing property identification number for the property (PIN) and property identification cards for ease of payment
				(iii) Verifying tax base and tax payment of taxpayers via surveys
				(iv) Collection of property tax and reassessment of the tax
Philippines	Property-based	Department of Finance	Bureau of Local Government Finance (BLGF)	Real property identification system for RPT purposes
			Local Government Units (LGUs)	Registration, administration, assessment, collection, and valuation
Thailand	Property-based	Ministry of Interior	Department of Local Administration (DLA)	Support local administrative organizations (LAOs) with
			- Division of Local Finance	(i) local administrative systems; (ii) developing tax and property maps to enhance local revenue collections (tax mapping); and (iii) training local personnel
			Local Administrative Organizations (LAOs)	Property tax administration and collection
		Ministry of Finance	Treasury Department	Property valuation/appraisal
Viet Nam	Person-based	Ministry of Natural Resources and Environment (MONRE)	General Department of Land Administration (GDLA)	Central database for all land-related information, including land assessment and valuation.
		Ministry of Finance	District or provincial tax office	Tax collection

Source: Authors' analysis based on data gathered from the four countries during the Workshop on Property Registration and Fiscal Cadastre, 9–10 May 2019, Manila.

Summary

Among the principal prerequisites for effective property taxation are adequate systems of property registration and fiscal cadastre that contain complete and up-to-date information about ownership, rights, actual use, sales prices, parcel boundaries, and other characteristics of immovable properties. Such systems can produce statistical data to support evidence-based revenue forecasting and decision-making on property tax reform, provide better estimates of the market value of properties, and improve the efficiency and effectiveness in administering and collecting property taxes. In this chapter, the customs and traditions related to land and property rights, the various systems of land registration, the institutional framework, and the fiscal cadastre system in the four countries are benchmarked.

With the exception of Viet Nam, the countries in this study recognize private ownership for both land and improvements; however, private ownership of land is in principle restricted to citizens, while private ownership of buildings and other structures is allowed for foreigners under certain conditions. In Viet Nam, land ownership rights are collective, and the state may grant land use rights to individuals, households, and organizations for different periods of time in accordance with the provisions of the Land Law.

The four countries have a title registry system, where the act of registration confers legal status and the registered property rights are, in most cases, guaranteed by the state. The function of their cadastral system is primary juridical, which is to serve as a legally recognized record of land tenure. In Thailand and Viet Nam, the cadastre is also established for fiscal purposes. Most countries have both a systematic and sporadic mechanism for land registration; however, Cambodia has recently moved away from sporadic land registration.

As shown in Tables 11 and 12, the functions and responsibilities for the maintenance of the land registry and fiscal cadastre, as well as the titling, valuation, surveying, and mapping of properties are often carried out by different tiers of government and organizations under different ministries. In Viet Nam, by contrast, these functions are integrated in one organization, with all land-related information being kept and maintained in a central government database under MONRE. For the assessment and collection of property taxes, Viet Nam's system relies on self-assessment and payment by land users at the local tax offices. In the other three countries, the information needed for property tax purposes has either been coordinated into one information system or arranged in such a way that different systems can exchange information.

In Cambodia, the records on taxpayers, properties, and payment history for the purpose of the immovable property tax and unused land tax are kept at the local tax branches, with a central fiscal database kept and maintained at the GDT. Like Viet Nam, Cambodia also has a person-based fiscal cadastre that is dependent on taxpayers to submit accurate declarations of their land and buildings holdings. When a transfer of hard title occurs, the district land offices of MLMUPC submits transfer documentation to the tax office for the collection of taxes. However, in the event of soft titles, tax authorities do not always receive such documentation from the local authorities. The GDT is currently in the process of improving data exchange with MLMUPC. In addition, the Cambodian government is conducting a study to adopt legislation that will provide the tax administration full powers to obtain information and data from relevant government institutions for tax purposes.

In the Philippines, which has a property-based fiscal cadastral system, all relevant data for purposes of real property taxation are being kept and maintained at the LGU level across the nation under a uniform classification system. By law, the registrar of deeds, the buildings officials and geodetic engineers (public or private) are mandated to periodically submit property-related information and registries to the LGUs.

In Thailand, there are three agencies involved in the fiscal cadastre development and maintenance: the Department of Land (cadastre), Treasury Department (property valuation or appraisal), and the Department of Local Government Administration (taxation mapping). With the recent introduction of the Land and Buildings Tax, the government has moved from a person-based to a property based-fiscal cadastre and is developing a new centralized property tax database to merge the data from the three departments.

A common concern raised among the countries is the lack of coordination between government organizations on the systematic exchange of records and/or the lack of data compatibility between the different information systems. The development of a modern land information system using computer technology has been a catalyst for closer coordination among organizations.

VI. Administrative Arrangements of Property Taxation

Introduction

The administration of property taxation encompasses (i) assessment and valuation of properties, and by extension thereof the effectiveness of the fiscal cadastre maintenance; (ii) billing, collection, and enforcement; (iii) appeal; and (iv) taxpayer service and education. How well these functions are performed, depends on a wide range of factors. As shown in Table 12, some of these administrative functions are carried out at different levels of government and sometimes at different ministries in the four countries. As such, ensuring a smooth data flow, as well as safeguarding the accountability of the different agencies and tiers of government for carrying out their respective responsibilities, are essential for the effective administration of the property tax.

Tax Assessment and Valuation

The process needed to produce good property tax assessment and valuation depends to a large extent on the accuracy of the fiscal cadastre, which should generate and record specific details about the taxable property (e.g., its actual use or classification, plot boundaries, building type, area, location), its value, and information about the taxpayer, including any eligibility for exemptions and reliefs. The development and maintenance of such data infrastructure is arguably the costliest facet of administering property taxation. A particular problem that exists in most developing countries is the scarcity of qualified property assessors. New technologies, such as computer-assisted mass appraisal (CAMA) system with geographic information system (GIS), satellite-aided mapping, cross-referencing data between intergovernmental agencies, and so forth, can lower the ongoing administrative costs and change the way governments administer their property taxes; however, implementing such technologies would require a significant upfront investment.

In Thailand, officers from the local administrative organizations (LAOs) carry out property survey and prepare the property assessment roll for taxation (which includes number, size, type, actual use, and value of properties; the latter based on the valuation by the officers in the provincial office of the Department of Treasury). The LAO issues public as well as individual notices to property owners to verify the results of the survey. Before 1 February each year, the LAO issues public notice on the assessed property value and tax rate. By the end of February each year, LAO conducts tax assessment and issues individual tax invoice to taxpayers. Taxpayers are required to pay the tax at the local authority office, a commercial bank or the post office by the end of April that year. In the event of nonpayment, the taxpayer will incur interest and penalties, and may be subject to the levying of distraint and seizure of property.

In the Philippines, the administration of the property tax falls under the control and responsibility of the LGUs, including the classification of real property (e.g., residential, agricultural, commercial, industrial), the determination of the assessment levels, tax rates, discounts, and penalties, but also the conversion of tax mapping information to individual property records and the collective assessment rolls, as well as the development and maintenance of basic records management system in a local assessment office (Miranda 2019). The provincial, city, or municipal assessor is responsible for the preparation and the maintenance of the assessment rolls, in which all real property, both taxable and exempt, in the locality is listed, valued, and assessed in the name of the property owner or administrator. However, taxpayers are required to assist in the tax assessment process, thereby reducing some of the LGUs' administrative costs. Property owners or administrators are required to prepare and file with the assessor a sworn statement declaring the current and fair market value of their property once every 3 years (Section 202, LGC 1991). In addition, taxpayers are required to submit proof of exemption of real property from taxation to the assessor when claiming for the application of an exemption. If the property owner fails to declare the property, the assessor may declare the property in the name of the defaulting owner or against an unknown owner (Section 204 of the LGC). Besides the taxpayer, other government agencies are required to furnish documentation ("Requirements in the Issuance of Tax Declaration") to the assessor, depending on the type of taxable property (e.g., untitled land, titled land, buildings, machines), such as a survey plan prepared by a licensed geodetic engineer and approved by the LMB, a certification from the Community Environment and Natural Resources Office that the land is within the alienable and disposable area, a certification from the barangay captain that the declarant is the present owner and occupant of the land, a certification of the adjoining owners duly sworn to by the barangay captain and/or the municipal mayor, a certified true copy of the title issued by the registrar of deeds, a copy of the approved building permit, building plan, and/or certificate of completion or certificate of occupancy permit from local officials concerned.

Cambodia and Viet Nam rely on a system of self-assessment, where taxpayers are required to register, declare, value, and calculate the assessments on their properties. In general, self-assessment can be an appealing procedure in countries with limited administrative capacity, as it is relatively easy to implement while keeping the administrative costs for governments low. However, such systems will inherently result in undertaxation, unless significant penalties are put in place and effectively enforced to deter nonreporting and underreporting. In Cambodia, taxpayers who have properties with a value higher than KHR100 million (approx. USD 25,000) and unused land have the obligation to file the immovable property tax, respectively the unused land tax, before 30 September each year at the local tax administration where those properties are located. Taxpayers are required to declare the size of land and building and calculate their tax liability based on the assessed market value per square meter as determined by the Ministry of Economy and Finance.[50] After submitting the tax declaration, the tax administration issues a property identification number (PIN) and card to the property owner for tax payment at a bank. The Property Tax Office from the General Department of Taxation has the authority to verify the declarations by taxpayers and contact property owners who have not done so to register, declare, and pay the property tax. In the event of incorrect declarations or nondeclarations, the Property Tax office shall issue penalties and reassess the property tax.

In a similar vein, taxpayers in Viet Nam are responsible for the registration, declaration, and payment of the land use taxes. Upon obtaining land use right, taxpayers are required to fill a one-off declaration form and submit it, together with a certification from the local commune, to the tax office. Taxpayers are not required to submit the declaration form again unless a transfer in land use right occurs. The tax is calculated by the local tax office by applying the tax rate on the taxable land area multiplied by the price per square meter fixed in the Land Price Table, which is revised every 5 years by the Province-level People's Committee. Since 2012, the law has provided the taxpayer the option to choose to pay the tax as a lump-sum payment for 5 years or annually.

---

[50] The valuation is prepared by the Immovable Properties Appraisal and Valuation Commission for the Tax on Immovable Property, by the Commission of Valuation of Unused Land for the Tax on Unused Land and submitted for approval to the Minister of Economy and Finance.

Table 13:   Administrative Arrangements for Assessment and Valuation

Country	Assessment		Valuation	
	Responsible Agency	System	Responsible Agency	System
Cambodia	Property Tax Office (GDT)	Self-assessment by taxpayer	Immovable Properties Appraisal and Valuation Commission	Self-declaration of value by taxpayer
			Commission of Valuation of Unused Land	Self-declaration of value by taxpayer
Philippines	Provincial, city or municipal assessor (LGU)	Assessment by provincial, city or municipal assessor with input from taxpayer and stakeholders	Local government units (LGUs)	Self-declaration (Sworn Statement declaring Market Value of Real Property) by taxpayer
Thailand	Local administrative organizations (LAOs)	Assessment by LAO	Provincial office of Treasury Department	Assessment by LAO
Viet Nam	District or provincial tax office (GDT)	Self-assessment by taxpayer	Province-level People's Committee (MONRE)	Self-declaration of value by taxpayer

Source: Authors' analysis based on data gathered from the four countries during the Workshop on Property Registration and Fiscal Cadastre, 9-10 May 2019, Manilla, and follow-up questionnaires and interviews.

Billing, Collection, and Enforcement

The functions of billing, collection, and enforcement of property taxes are often performed by the local authorities, who are (in most cases) the recipients of the tax revenues and therefore have a direct interest. In addition, collection at the local level also provides convenience to taxpayers with collection points close to their homes.

In the Philippines, the provinces and cities, including the municipalities within the Metropolitan Manila area, are primarily responsible for the administration of the Real Property Tax (RPT). The collection and enforcement of the property tax is the responsibility of the provincial, city, or municipal treasurer, who receives the assessment roll from the provincial, city, or municipal assessor. All revenue collected from the RPT goes directly to the budget of the LGU. In Thailand, the property tax is also administered and collected by local authorities and the collected tax goes directly to the local budget. In Cambodia all taxes are collected and administered by the state through the General Department of Taxation (GDT). As stipulated under Section 2 of the Immovable Property Tax of the Law on Financial Management for the year 2010 and under the *Prakas* 371 and Notification 006 on the Immovable Property Tax issued by the MEF in 2011, the property tax revenue is assigned to the subnational administrative budget (capital, provinces, cities, districts, *khans*, communes, *sangkats*) for the purpose of its regional development. Similarly, in Viet Nam, revenues from the agricultural land use tax and the non-agricultural land use tax are collected by the district or provincial tax office of the GDT. Subnational governments are allowed to retain 100% of the property tax revenue (Trung et al. 2015).

All countries issue tax notices annually to remind taxpayers of their obligation to pay the property tax, although not every country issues individual bills. Countries that rely on self-assessment and self-declaration do not necessarily have an individual billing system in place. In Cambodia, the GDT issues public notifications to remind taxpayers to file their annual property tax declaration and to pay the tax at any tax branch or at any branch of the financial institutions authorized to collect tax payments (e.g., Canadia Bank, Acleda Bank, Wing [Cambodia] Limited

Specialized Bank) by providing the tax payment receipt of the previous year before the deadline of 30 September each year. In the future, the GDT intends to send all notifications related to property tax together with the utility bill to the taxpayers individually. In Viet Nam, land users receive individual tax notices from the tax authorities on the amount of tax they need to pay. If taxpayers have opted to pay the tax quinquennially, the tax authorities will issue a notification for a lump-sum payment. In the Philippines, the city or municipal treasurer posts a public notice of the dates when the tax may be paid without interest at a visible and publicly accessible place at the city or municipal hall and publishes that notification in a newspaper of general circulation in the locality once a week for two consecutive weeks before 31 January each year. In Thailand, LAO issues both public and individual notices to encourage property owners to verify the results of the property surveys, but the tax assessments and tax invoices are issued to taxpayers individually.

Some countries have enforcement measures in place for the central government to ensure proper tax collection by local authorities. In the Philippines, any local treasurer or his or her deputy who fails to issue or execute the warrant of levy within 1 year from the time the tax becomes delinquent or within 30 days from the date of the issuance thereof, or who is found guilty of abusing the exercise thereof in an administrative or judicial proceeding, shall be dismissed from the service (Section 259 of the LGC 1991). Similarly in Thailand, local authorities who fail to collect the property tax may be penalized by the auditor general.

Table 14:   Administrative Arrangements for Billing, Collection, and Enforcement

Country	Billing	Collection	Enforcement
Cambodia	Public notifications; self-declaration	General Department of Taxation (GDT)	General Department of Taxation (GDT)
Philippines	Public notifications; Provincial, city or municipal treasurer (LGU)	Provincial, city or municipal treasurer (LGU)	Provincial, city or municipal treasurer (LGU)
Thailand	Local administrative organizations (LAOs)	Local administrative organizations (LAOs)	Local administrative organizations (LAOs)
Viet Nam	Individual notices; self-declaration	District or provincial tax office (GDT)	District or provincial tax office (GDT)

Source: Authors, based on data gathered from the four countries during the Workshop on Property Registration and Fiscal Cadastre, 9–10 May 2019, Manila, and follow-up questionnaires and interviews.

Appeal

All countries have an appeals system in place for taxpayers to challenge the tax assessment and property valuation.

In Cambodia, taxpayers can lodge a complaint with the local tax officials. If the dispute cannot be resolved, the taxpayer can discuss their case with the tax branch of the provincial *khan*, and subsequently with the GDT, the Committee on Tax Arbitration and finally the court.

In the Philippines, taxpayers can appeal before the local board regarding the tax assessment by the provincial, city, or municipal assessor or the collection by the provincial, city, or municipal treasurer. However, no protest or appeal shall be entertained unless the taxpayer first pays the RPT, with the words "PAID UNDER PROTEST" written on the tax receipt (Section 252 of the LGC 1991). The Central Board of Assessment Appeals has exclusive jurisdiction to hear and decide all appeals from the decisions, orders, and resolutions of the local boards involving contested assessments of real properties, claims for tax refund, and/or tax credits or overpayments of taxes (Sections 229–230 of the LGC 1991).

In Thailand, a taxpayer can lodge a complaint on the assessment and collection on the property tax by sending a complaint letter to LAO within 30 days after receiving the tax assessment invoice. The LAO has 60 days to consider and inform the taxpayer of its decision, against which the taxpayer may appeal before the Provincial Appeal Committee. If the taxpayer is still dissatisfied with the verdict, he or she can bring the case to the Court of Justice within 30 days. Complaints against the valuation of properties, however, have to be lodged before the Property Valuation Committee through either the Land Registration Office or the Department of Treasury, as property valuation operates under the Land Code.

Similarly, in Viet Nam taxpayers may lodge complaints with the tax administration agencies under the Law on Tax Administration on the assessment and collection of taxes. For the valuation of properties, however, the provincial-level natural resources and environment departments are responsible.

Taxpayer Service and Education

Taxpayer service and education play an important role in raising taxpayers' voluntary compliance level and enhance the effectiveness of revenue collection. The four countries in this study initiated different strategic approaches.

In 2016, the GDT of Cambodia launched the Property Survey Working Group to assist property owners in the registration of property information and to issue property identification cards directly at the address of the owner after completing the registration. To improve tax compliance, the GDT engages in taxpayer education programs, for example, conducting seminars and preparing guidance notes, with the aim to teach taxpayers about their tax rights, responsibilities, and legal requirements. In addition, to improve the ease of payment for taxpayers, the MEF has signed agreements with financial institutions to facilitate in the collection of tax payments, including using their online banking systems and mobile money platforms.[51]

Viet Nam has established "one-stop" shops throughout the country to improve taxpayer service and ease of self-declarations and tax payment at the different levels of government. Land users can access different types of government services at the one-stop shops, including exchange and transfer of land use rights, designation of land use, and local tax collection and fees.[52] In addition, tax authorities at all levels and tax agents in Viet Nam provide technical support to taxpayers on an ad hoc basis.

In the Philippines, different LGUs have launched programs to improve the ease of payment of RPT. The Local Government of Quezon City, for example, through its partnership with the United States Agency for International Development (USAID) under the Scaling Innovations through Mobile Money project, has developed an online payment system that enables its residents to pay their RPT via mobile phone using the G-Cash facility. In addition, taxpayers may receive discounts when paying the tax before the due date.

---

[51] C. Sokhorng. 2016. Gov't taps Wing for tax collection. *The Phnom Penh Post.* 5 March.
[52] World Bank. 2017. *One-Stop Shops in Vietnam, Changing the Face of Public Administration for Citizen and Business through a Single Door to Multiple Services.* Washington, DC.

Resources: Funding, Staffing, and Information Technology Support

The effective administration of property taxes requires a significant amount of resources. For many DMCs, budgetary constraints, lack of human resources (in particular, qualified property assessors or valuators), and fragmented data infrastructure are often cited as some of the main challenges for administering the property tax. The emergence of modern digital technologies, in particular GIS, satellite mapping, and CAMA system, has made it easier for governments to locate and record properties, maintain an up-to-date fiscal cadastre, and produce better valuations. Introducing such technologies, as well as developing training programs for assessors, would require a significant upfront investment.

The amount of resources needed for administering a property tax depends on the design of the tax system, for example, the scope and coverage of the tax, area-based or value-based, the frequency of revaluations, but also the availability of cadastral data and the use of information technology systems (such as land information system and CAMA system with GIS) supporting the valuation and administration of the property tax. The degree of fiscal decentralization may also have an impact on the demand for resources: centralized administrations may benefit from the advantages in economies of scale, whereas in highly decentralized structures of governments local officers and politicians may have better information at their disposal as they are closer to local needs and demands.

Comparing the administrative costs between the four countries is extremely difficult, as little comparable statistical data are available at the time of writing of this report. As some countries (e.g., Viet Nam and Cambodia) do not separate the property tax-related costs from other operational costs in the governmental budgeting and accounting system, analyzing the funding and staffing costs at the different levels of government can be challenging. On the other end of the spectrum, the Philippines has developed the Electronic Statement of Receipts and Expenditures system (eSRE) to monitor the LGUs' financial performance that includes unique indicators. One is the ratio of Total Revenue Office Operations Costs to Total Revenues Collected, which reflects the full cost-effectiveness of the local revenue generation efforts of an LGU and accounts not only the collection costs of the revenue offices (i.e., Treasury and Assessors Offices), but also the costs of subsidizing other operations of these offices or revenue centers (e.g., disbursement). The other indicator is the Real Property Tax Accomplishment Rate, which determines the ratio of the collected RPT to the total RPT due for a year as estimated from the assessed value of taxable real properties.[53] In 2018, the net RPT collection efficiency was reported at 72.3% (Miranda 2019). These data can help LGUs make informed decisions on capacity needs and the allocation of resources to the administration of the RPT in order to maximize its revenue potential.

Monitoring Performance

As suggested by Kaplan and Norton,: "You can't improve what you can't measure and if you cannot measure it, you cannot manage it" (Kaplan and Norton 1996). To ensure the effective implementation and administration of a property tax, the development of a monitoring system based on quantitative performance indicators is essential. This would ideally include regular assessments of coverage of the tax register, valuation performance, and collection efficiency (Norregaard 2013).

---

[53] Bureau of Local Government Finance (BLGF). 2015. Local Public Financial Management Tools for the Electronic Statement of Receipts and Expenditures (eSRE).

From the four countries in this study, the Philippines has the most comprehensive performance-monitoring system in place. On 12 July 2018, the Department of Budget and Management, the Department of Finance, and the Department of the Interior and Local Government signed a joint memorandum[54] to adopt a comprehensive reporting of LGU fiscal data of local treasurers, assessors, budget officers and accountants, the so-called "LGU Integrated Financial Tools or LIFT System." Maintained by the BLGF, the system captures (i) eSRE of local treasurers, (ii) quarterly reporting of real property assessments of assessors, (iii) expenditure tagging and management, (iv) harmonized eSRE with accounting records, and (v) consolidated financial statements of *barangays* or villages. Under this system, the revenue performance of the RPT can be closely monitored.[55] Cambodia is also developing a set of key performance indicators and targets under the Revenue Mobilization Strategy 2019–2023 with the aim to monitor the implementation of the administrative reform of the property tax.

Summary

The administration of property taxation encompasses

- assessment and valuation of properties,
- billing, collection and enforcement,
- appeal, and
- taxpayer service and education.

Tax Assessment and Valuation

The process needed to produce accurate property tax assessment and valuation depends, to a large extent, on the administrative capacity and resources to develop and maintain an effective fiscal cadastral system. A problem in most developing countries is the scarcity of qualified property assessors. To address this issue, some countries rely on a system of self-assessment, where the taxpayer is responsible for the registration, declaration, valuation, and payment of the tax. This can be an attractive procedure in countries with limited administrative capacity, as it is relatively easy to implement while keeping the administrative costs for governments low. However, such systems will inherently result in undertaxation, unless significant penalties are put in place and effectively enforced to deter non-reporting and underreporting. Cambodia and Viet Nam have a system of self-assessment. In the Philippines, taxpayers are required to assist in the tax assessment and valuation process, including declaring the current and fair market value of their property once every 3 years in a sworn statement and submitting proof of exemption of RPT when claiming such. However, the preparation and maintenance of the assessment rolls, including the valuation of properties, fall under the responsibility of the LGUs, and as part of the assessment process different government agencies are mandated by law to periodically furnish land-related documentations and registries to the assessor. In Thailand, officers from the LAOs carry out property survey and prepare the property assessment roll, with valuations from the Department of Treasury. The role of taxpayers in this process is limited to the verification of the survey results and tax payment.

---

[54] Joint Memorandum Circular (JMC), No. 2018-1, 12 July 2018.
[55] P.P. Quizon. 2019. *Philippines Property Tax Management and Statistics.* Presentation prepared for the ADB Workshop on Property Tax: Property Registration and Fiscal Cadastre. Manila. 9–10 May.

Billing, Collection, and Enforcement

The functions of billing, collection, and enforcement of property taxes are often performed by the local authorities, who are the recipients of the tax revenues and therefore have a direct interest in getting taxpayers to pay their taxes. All countries in this study issue public and/or individual tax notices annually to remind taxpayers of their obligation to pay the property tax. In Cambodia and Viet Nam, the local tax offices of the GDT are responsible for the collection and enforcement of the property tax. In the Philippines and Thailand, where the administration and collection of property taxes are decentralized, local authorities can be penalized for failure to collect the tax.

Appeal

To safeguard taxpayer's rights, all countries have an appeal system in place by which a taxpayer may challenge the tax assessment or valuation. In most cases, the first step is to lodge a complaint to the local authority or tax office responsible for the assessment or valuation. If the dispute cannot be resolved, taxpayers can appeal before the courts and tribunals.

Taxpayer Service and Education

Taxpayer service and education play an important role in improving taxpayers' voluntary compliance and enhancing the effectiveness of revenue collection. Common strategies include improving the ease of payment using online banking systems and mobile money platforms. Some countries provide incentives such as discounts for timely payment.

The administration of property taxes requires a significant amount of resources. For many countries, budgetary constraints, lack of human resources (in particular, qualified property assessors) and fragmented data infrastructure are often cited as some of the main challenges for efficient property tax administration. However, most countries do not have a performance monitoring system in place to effectively assess the coverage, valuation, and collection ratios of the tax. Developing such a system, based on quantitative performance indicators, can facilitate accountability and contribute to governments' strategies for effective implementation and administration of the property tax.

VII. Conclusions and the Way Forward

This study provides an analysis of the property tax regime in Cambodia, the Philippines, Thailand, and Viet Nam in terms of the scope for increasing domestic resource mobilization, the contribution to government strategies, the coherence with other systems and government functions related to land management, the design of the tax, and the effectiveness of the administration. This analysis can serve as a basis for DMCs to compare, evaluate, and improve the performance of property taxation and to stimulate consideration of reform opportunities.

Domestic Resource Mobilization

Property taxation has significant revenue potential and can play an important role in DMC governments' strategy for sustainable domestic resource mobilization. Existing recurrent property taxes do not emerge as an important source of revenue in the four countries, with the lowest revenue yield reported in Viet Nam (0.024% of GDP) and the highest in the Philippines (0.38% of GDP) in 2017. The low performance can be contributed to policy design issues, such as a narrow tax base, low effective tax rates, and below market-price valuations. In addition, gaps in financial and human resources, data infrastructure and technical applications have an adverse impact on the administrative and operational capacity for effective implementation and enforcement of the property tax.

There is substantial scope for increasing revenues, and the countries in this study have initiated different reform strategies to enhance the performance of the property tax system. Cambodia has undertaken an administrative reform aimed at improving the registration and valuation of properties in the tax roll, while strengthening enforcement and compliance of the property tax. The Philippines' reform focuses on professionalizing the valuation process of real properties by adopting "internationally accepted valuation standards, concepts, principles, and practices"[56] and recentralizing the approval of SMVs by LGUs back to the secretary of the Department of Finance. Thailand has recently enacted the new Land and Building Tax Act to replace the low-performing 1932 Building and Land Tax and the 1965 Land Development Tax. With, among others, a broader tax base, higher rates for vacant land, and moving away from a rental value to toward a market value approach, the new tax is expected to yield THB40 billion after a phase-in period of 3 years, an increase of 17% in tax revenue. Viet Nam is also considering introducing a new property tax law by merging the current agricultural and non-agricultural land use taxes and moving from a land-only tax (site value taxation) toward a more traditional recurrent property tax that includes both land and improvements.

These reform initiatives are a positive step toward sustainable revenue mobilization. To ensure the effective implementation of the ongoing reform efforts, governments should implement a monitoring system based on quantitative performance indicators, which should ideally include regular assessments of coverage of the tax

---

56 House Bill No. 4664, Article I, Section 2 (Declaration of Policy and Objectives).

register, valuation performance, and collection efficiency (Norregaard 2013). Such a monitoring system would contribute to an environment of data-driven decision-making.

Recommendations on the Way Forward

A strategy for achieving sustainable increased revenues from property tax reform must be carefully designed to tailor to the individual country's particular circumstances and applied gradually to avoid sudden impacts, particularly on vulnerable taxpayers and compensating measures that may be required for them. Increasing the property tax revenue to 1% (or more) of GDP would deliver significant benefits to the country and setting such a goal for, say, 5–10 years hence could establish a context for the continuous improvement of the system and administration of property tax.

From the assessment of the main design features of property taxation (Chapter 4), property registration and fiscal cadastre (Chapter 5), and administrative arrangements (Chapter 6) in the four countries, the following factors can be addressed to improve revenue performance.

A. Policy Design Issues

1. **Broaden the tax base.** All countries have a range of tax benefits in their tax code, such as exemptions for government properties and historic and cultural sites, but also tax incentives for businesses operating in e-zones and tax reliefs to protect vulnerable taxpayers (e.g., by using basic property tax thresholds or exempting owner-occupied housing). These tax benefits significantly narrow the tax base and their objectives may be achieved in other ways.

2. **Increase effective rates.** The statutory rates are generally low, with the effective rates even lower. Increases can be phased in over a number of years.

3. **Use up-to-date market-price valuations.** Often assessed values do not reflect the current market value, either by design or due to constraints in administrative capacities. Regular revaluation of property is necessary to maintain buoyancy and to ensure fairness.

B. Cadastral Record-Keeping Issues

1. **Modernize data infrastructure.** Among the principal prerequisites for effective property taxation are adequate systems of property registration and fiscal cadastre that contain complete and up-to-date information about ownership, rights, actual use, sales prices, parcel boundaries, and other characteristics of immovable properties. Such systems can produce statistical data to support evidence-based revenue forecasting and decision-making on property tax reform, provide better estimates of the market value of properties, and improve the efficiency and effectiveness in administering and collecting property taxes. In most countries, the functions and responsibilities for the maintenance of the land registry and fiscal cadastre, as well as the titling, valuation, surveying, and mapping of properties, are carried out by different tiers of government and organizations under different ministries, resulting in fragmented data keeping.

2. **Cooperation in government data sharing.** A common concern raised among the countries is the lack of coordination between government organizations on the systematic exchange of records and/or the lack of data compatibility between the different information systems. Ensuring a smooth data flow, as well as safeguarding accountability of the different government institutions involved, are essential for the effective administration of the property tax.

3. **Secure reliable data on recent sales prices.** Market value assessment is based on comparable sales prices between a willing buyer and a willing seller in an arm's length transaction. In some instances, reliable data on recent sales and listing prices are not readily available due to the absence of developed property markets. As markets develop especially in urban areas, action is needed to capture actual data and counter the underreporting of transactions to evade property transfer taxes.

C. Administrative Issues

1. **Strengthen financial and human resources.** Effective implementation of property taxation requires adequate administrative capacity (i.e., sufficient financial and human resources). A common issue problem in developing countries is the scarcity of qualified property assessors. New technologies, such as CAMA system with GIS, satellite-aided mapping, and cross-referencing data between intergovernmental agencies, can lower the ongoing administrative costs and change the way governments administer their property taxes. However, implementing such technologies would require a significant upfront investment.

2. **Improve taxpayer compliance.** Most countries in this study rely on a system of self-assessment, where taxpayers are required to register, declare, value, and/or calculate the assessments on their properties. Self-assessment can be an appealing procedure, particularly in countries with limited administrative capacity, as it is relatively easy to implement while keeping the administrative costs for governments low. However, such systems will inherently result in undertaxation, unless significant penalties are put in place and effectively enforced to deter nonreporting and underreporting.

3. **Implement standards for valuation practices.** Valuation is a major administrative challenge in virtually all developing countries. Setting and monitoring common standards will protect revenues and avoid regional disparities in property valuation.

Contributing to Other Government Strategies

This report concentrates on the revenue-raising goals of property taxation and recognizes that other government strategies may be supported by the design of property taxation. It is noted that property tax can be a policy instrument to promote efficient land use management, for example, by increased tax rates for unused property and that this may also be supportive of infrastructure development. It is generally accepted that a well-designed property tax based on market valuations can have an effect on stabilization of residential property prices and can play a role in land value capture. The relationship with fiscal decentralization is more nuanced: while there is scope for property tax to make a bigger contribution to local government finance, fiscal decentralization has not been a driver of resource mobilization in low-income developing countries. These issues are worth further attention and in particular the issue of land value capture is increasingly relevant for developing countries in the region experiencing accelerated development in urban areas.

The relationship between property taxation and land management brings into play the opportunities that e-government approaches to data and technology can provide. We note and welcome the investigation of possible projects to support the coordinated development of comprehensive land management information systems that can provide a sound basis for a fiscal cadastre and be deployed for a range of purposes encompassing land and resource management and social and environmental protection.

References

A. Abiad, K. Farrin, and C. Hale. 2019. Sustaining Transit Investment in Asia's Cities, A Beneficiary-Funding and Land Value Capture Perspective. Manila: Asian Development Bank. https://www.adb.org/sites/default/files/publication/496991/sustaining-transit-investment-asia-cities.pdf.

R. Almy and M. Cusack. 2017. Workable Solutions for Property Tax Reform. Paper prepared for the 2017 World Bank conference on Land and Poverty. Washington, DC. March 20–24.

Asian Development Bank (ADB). 2018. Fiscal Decentralization Reform in Cambodia, Progress over the past decade and opportunities. Manila. https://www.adb.org/sites/default/files/publication/479961/fiscal-decentralization-reform-cambodia.pdf.

———. 2018. Valuation reform project concept note brief. No. PHI 52173-001. Manila. https://www.adb.org/sites/default/files/linked-documents/52173-001-sd-02.pdf.

———. 2018. Strategy 2030: Achieving a Prosperous, Inclusive, Resilient, and Sustainable Asia and the Pacific. Manila.

R. Bahl and J. Martinez-Vazquez. 2007. The Property Tax in Developing Countries: Current Practice and Prospects, Lincoln Institute of Land Policy Working Paper. No. WP07RB1. Cambridge: Lincoln Institute of Land Policy.

R. Bahl and J. Martinez-Vazquez. 2008. The Determinants of Revenue Performance. In Bahl, Martinez-Vazquez and Youngman, eds. Making the Property Tax Work: Experiences in Developing and Transitional Countries, Cambridge: Lincoln Institute of Land Policy.

R. Bahl. 2009. Property Tax Reform in Developing and Transition Countries. USAID. https://www.joserobertoafonso.com.br/attachment/6688

R.M. Bird and F. Vaillancourt. 1998. Fiscal decentralization in developing countries: An overview. In Bird and Vaillancourt, eds. Fiscal Decentralization in Developing Countries. Cambridge: Cambridge University Press.

R.M. Bird and E. Slack. 2002. Land and Property Taxation Around the World: A Review. Washington, DC: World Bank. http://www1.worldbank.org/publicsector/decentralization/June2003Seminar/LandPropertyTaxation.pdf.

R.M. Bird and E. Slack. 2004. International Handbook on Land and Property Taxation. Cheltenham: Edward Elgar Publishing Inc.

H. Blöchliger. 2015. Reforming the Tax on Immovable Property: Taking Care of the Unloved. OECD Economics Department Working Papers. No. 1205. Paris: OECD. https://www.oecd-ilibrary.org/economics/reforming-the-tax-on-immovable-property_5js30tw0n7kg-en.

C. Boonyanate. 2019. Land and Building Tax. Presentation prepared for the ADB Conference on Property Tax Reform and Domestic Resource Mobilization in Asia and the Pacific Region. Manila. 16–18 September.

N. Brandt. 2014. Greening the Property Tax. OECD Working Papers on Fiscal Federalism, No. 17. Paris: OECD. https://www.oecd-ilibrary.org/taxation/greening-the-property-tax_5jz5pzw9mwzn-en.

B. Brys et al. 2016. Tax Design for Inclusive Economic Growth. *OECD Taxation Working Papers.* No. 26. Paris: OECD. https://www.oecd-ilibrary.org/taxation/tax-design-for-inclusive-economic-growth_5jlv74ggk0g7-en.

Centre for Spatial Data Infrastructures and Land Administration (CSDILA). 2019. Cadastral Template 2.0, Cambodia. http://cadastraltemplate.org/cambodia.php (accessed on 19 August 2019).

———. 2019. Cadastral Template 2.0, Philippines. http://cadastraltemplate.org/cadastraltemplate/philippines.php (accessed on 19 August 2019).

———. 2019. Cadastral Template 2.0, Thailand. http://cadastraltemplate.org/thailand.php (accessed on 19 August 2019).

I. Chatry and R.C. Vincent. 2019. A global view of sub-national governments in Asia: Structure and finance. In Kim and Dougherty, eds. *Fiscal Decentralisation and Inclusive Growth in Asia,* OECD Fiscal Federalism Studies. Paris: OECD.

P. Collier et al. 2017. Land and property taxes: Exploiting untapped municipal revenues, IGC Policy Brief. https://www.theigc.org/wp-content/uploads/2017/08/Land-and-property-taxes-policy-brief_updated.pdf.

G.C. Cornia. 2013. Tax Criteria: The Design and Policy Advantages of a Property Tax. In McCluskey, Cornia and Walters, eds. A Primer on Property Tax: Administration and Policy. West Sussex: Blackwell Publishing Ltd.

ECE. 1996. Land Administration Guidelines. No. ECE/HBP/96, Geneva: Economic Commission for Europe/United Nations. http://www.unece.org/fileadmin/DAM/hlm/documents/Publications/land.administration.guidelines.e.pdf.

European Commission. 2019. Taxation Trends in the European Union, Data for the EU Member States, Iceland and Norway. Luxembourg: Publication Office of the European Union. https://ec.europa.eu/taxation_customs/sites/taxation/files/taxation_trends_report_2019.pdf.

S. Fung and B. McAuley. 2020. Cambodia's Property Tax Reform, Policy Consideration Toward Sustained Revenue Mobilization. The Governance Brief. Issue 38. Manila: Asian Development Bank. https://www.adb.org/sites/default/files/publication/561136/governance-brief-038-cambodia-property-tax-reform.pdf.

Government of the Philippines. 2015. Local Public Financial Management Tools for the Electronic Statement of Receipts and Expenditures (eSRE). Manila. http://blgf.gov.ph/wp-content/uploads/2017/02/LocalPublicFinancialManagementToolsfortheeSREv4.pdf.

———. 2019. LGUs losing P30.5-B revenues to outdated real property valuation. Manila. http://taxreform.dof.gov.ph/news_and_updates/lgus-losing-p30-5-b-revenues-to-outdated-real-property-valuation/.

———. 2019. Package 3: Real property valuation reform. Manila. http://taxreform.dof.gov.ph/presentations-and-references/ctrp-package-3-real-property-valuation-reform-1-page-briefer/.

———. 2020. House Bill No. 4664: Real property valuation (18th Congress). Manila. https://taxreform.dof.gov.ph/presentations-and-references/house-bill-no-4664-real-property-valuation-18th-congress/.

Government of Viet Nam. *Viet Nam Sustainable Development Strategy for 2011–2020*. Ha Noi. http://www.vietnam.gov.vn/portal/page/portal/English/strategies/strategiesdetails?categoryId=30&articleId=10050825.

C. von Haldenwang. 2015. *The Political Cost of Local Revenue Mobilisation: Decentralisation of Property Tax in Indonesia SSRN*. http://ssrn.com/abstract=2579598.

S. Hem. 2019. The Land Registration Process in Cambodia: Background, Procedures, and Outcomes. Cambodian J. Int. Stud. 3. https://uc.edu.kh/CJIS/Article_Land%20Registration%20in%20Cambodia_2019_HS.pdf.

J.L.G. Henssen. 1995. Basic principles of the main cadastral systems in the world. Proceedings of the One Day Seminar held during the Annual Meeting of Commission 7 of the International Federation of Surveyors (FIG). Delft. 16 May.

The International Federation of Surveyors. 1995. FIG Statement on the Cadastre. FIG Publication. No. 11. https://www.fig.net/resources/publications/figpub/pub11/figpub11.asp.

International Monetary Fund. 2014. *Governance Finance Statistics Manual 2014 (GFSM)*. Washington, DC. https://www.imf.org/external/Pubs/FT/GFS/Manual/2014/gfsfinal.pdf.

S.F. Joireman and J. Brown. 2013. Property: Human Right or Commodity? *Journal of Human Rights*. 12 (2). https://scholarship.richmond.edu/cgi/viewcontent.cgi?referer=https://www.google.com/&httpsredir=1&article=1070&context=polisci-faculty-publications.

R.S. Kaplan and D.P. Norton. 1996. *The Balanced Scorecard: Translating Strategy Into Action*. Boston: Harvard Business School Press.

R. Kelly. 2013. Property Tax Collection and Enforcement. In McCluskey, Cornia and Walters, eds. A Primer on Property Tax: Administration and Policy. West Sussex: Blackwell Publishing Ltd.

D. Laovakul. 2016. Property Tax in Thailand: An Assessment and Policy Implications. Thammasat Review of Economic and Social Policy. 2 (1). http://www.tresp.econ.tu.ac.th/paper/vol2/5_Duangmanee%20Laovakul.pdf.

T.H. Loan and W.J. McCluskey. 2010. Property Tax in Vietnam: The Potential for Reform. Journal of Property Tax Assessment & Administration. 7 (1). https://pure.ulster.ac.uk/ws/portalfiles/portal/11276037/Viet_PropTax_Reform_032210_%282%29.pdf.

J. Martinez-Vazquez, L. Noiset, and M. Rider. 2010. Assignment of the Property Tax: Should Developing Countries Follow the Conventional View? In Bahl, Martinez-Vazquez and Youngman, eds. Challenging the Conventional Wisdom on the Property Tax. Cambridge: Lincoln Institute of Land Policy.

R. Maurer and A. Paugam. 2000. Reform Toward Ad Valorem Property Tax in Transition Economies: Fiscal and Land Use Benefits. *Land and Real Estate Initiative, Background Series 13*. Washington, DC: World Bank.

J.L. Mikesell. 2013. Administration of Local Taxes: An International Review of Practices and Issues for Enhancing Fiscal Autonomy. In McCluskey, Cornia and Walters, eds. A Primer on Property Tax: Administration and Policy. West Sussex: Blackwell Publishing Ltd.

B.L. Miranda. 2019. Property Taxation: Philippine Context. Presentation prepared for the ADB Conference on Property Tax Reform and Domestic Resource Mobilization in Asia and the Pacific Region. Manila. 16–18 September.

P.J. Morgan and L.Q. Trinh. 2016. Fiscal Decentralization and Local Budget Deficits in Viet Nam: An Empirical Analysis. ADBI Working Paper. No. 613. Tokyo: Asian Development Bank Institute. https://www.adb.org/publications/fiscal-decentralization-local-budget-deficits-viet-nam.

J. Muellbauer. 2005. Property Taxation and the Economy After the Barker Review. The Economic Journal. 115 (502). http://citeseerx.ist.psu.edu/viewdoc/download?doi=10.1.1.149.8037&rep=rep1&type=pdf.

National Tax Research Center. 2016. Guide to Philippines Taxes, Chapter XI Local Taxes. https://ntrc.gov.ph/images/Publications/guide-to-philippine-taxes-2016/local-taxes.pdf.

J. Norregaard. 2013. Taxing Immovable Property: Revenue Potential and Implementation Challenges. IMF Working Paper. No. WP/13/129. Washington, DC: International Monetary Fund. https://www.imf.org/external/pubs/ft/wp/2013/wp13129.pdf.

Organisation of Economic Co-operation and Development (OECD). 2010. Tax Policy Reform and Economic Growth. OECD Tax Policy Studies. No. 20. Paris: OECD. https://www.oecd.org/ctp/tax-policy/tax-policy-reform-and-economic-growth-9789264091085-en.htm.

———. 2016. Fiscal Federalism 2016: Making Decentralisation Work. Paris: OECD Publishing. https://www.oecd.org/publications/fiscal-federalism-2016-9789264254053-en.htm.

———. 2018. Revenue Statistics in Asian and Pacific Economies. Paris: OECD Publishing. https://doi.org/10.1787/9789264308091-en.

———. 2018. Revenue Statistics 1965–2017, Interpretative Guide. Paris: OECD Publishing. https://www.oecd.org/tax/tax-policy/oecd-classification-taxes-interpretative-guide.pdf.

———. 2019. Revenue Statistics in Asian and Pacific Economies 1990–2017. Paris: OECD Publishing. https://www.oecd-ilibrary.org/sites/b614e035-en/index.html?itemId=/content/publication/b614e035-en.

OECD/United Cities and Local Governments (UCLG). 2016. Subnational Governments Around the World, Part III Country Profiles. http://www.oecd.org/cfe/regional-policy/sngs-around-the-world.htm.

———. 2019. 2019 Report of the World Observatory on Subnational Government Finance and Investment – Country Profiles. http://www.sng-wofi.org/publications/SNGWOFI_2019_report_country_profiles.pdf.

P.P. Quizon. 2019. Philippines Property Tax Management and Statistics. Presentation prepared for the ADB Workshop on Property Tax: Property Registration and Fiscal Cadastre. Manila. 9–10 May.

———. 2019. *The Philippines Valuation Reform*. Presentation prepared for the ADB Conference on Property Tax Reform and Domestic Resource Mobilization in Asia and the Pacific Region. Manila. 16–18 September.

J.K. Rosengard. 1998. Property Tax Reform in Developing Countries. New York: Springer Science+Business Media LLC.

———. 2013. The Tax Everyone Loves to Hate: Principles of Property Tax Reform. In McCluskey, Cornia and Walters, eds. A Primer on Property Tax: Administration and Policy. West Sussex: Blackwell Publishing Ltd.

M. Roth and N. McCarthy. 2013. Land Tenure, Property Rights, and Economic Growth in Rural Areas. USAID Issue Brief. U.S. Agency for International Development. https://www.land-links.org/wp-content/uploads/2016/09/USAID_Land_Tenure_Economic_Growth_Issue_Brief-061214-1.pdf.

M. Salm. 2017. Property Tax in BRICS Megacities: Local Government Financing and Financial Sustainability. Cham: Springer International Publishing AG.

W.S. Scott. 1914. Western Weekly Reports. Vol. VI March–September. Calgary: Burroughs & Co Limited.

G.D. Shukla, D.M. Pham, M. Engelschalk and T.M. Le, eds. 2011. Tax Reform in Vietnam: Toward a More Efficient and Equitable System. Washington, DC: The World Bank. https://openknowledge.worldbank.org/bitstream/handle/10986/26851/663170WP0TaxPo00Box365757B00PUBLIC0.pdf?sequence=1.

E. Slack and R.M. Bird. 2014. The Political Economy of Property Tax Reform. OECD Working Papers on Fiscal Federalism, No. 18. Paris: OECD Publishing. https://munkschool.utoronto.ca/imfg/uploads/271/oecdwp18.pdf.

L.Q. Trung et al. 2015. *The Distribution of Powers and Responsibilities Affecting Forests, Land Use, and REDD+ Across Levels and Sectors in Vietnam: A Legal Study* Occasional Paper 137. Bogor: Center for International Forestry Research. http://www.cifor.org/publications/pdf_files/OccPapers/OP-137.pdf.

UN-HABITAT. 2011. Land and Property Tax: A Policy Guide. Nairobi: United Nations Human Settlements Programme. http://www.ipti.org/wp-content/uploads/2017/06/United-Nations-Land-and-Property-Tax-A-Policy-Guide-2011.pdf.

N. Usui. 2007. Critical Issues of Fiscal Decentralization. *ERD Technical Note.* No. 2. Manila: Asian Development Bank. https://www.adb.org/publications/critical-issues-fiscal-decentralization.

S. Varanyuwatana. 2004. Property Tax in Thailand. In R.M. Bird and E. Slack, eds. International Handbook of Land and Property Taxation. Cheltenham: Edward Elgar Publishing.

I.P. Williamson. 1985. Cadastres and Land Information Systems in Common Law Jurisdictions. Survey Review. 28 (217) pp. 114-129.

———. 1997. The justification of cadastral systems in developing countries. Geomatica. 51 (1) pp. 21-36.

World Bank. 2017. One-Stop Shops in Vietnam, Changing the Face of Public Administration for Citizen and Business through a Single Door to Multiple Services. https://openknowledge.worldbank.org/bitstream/handle/10986/27487/117081-BRI-P157228-PUBLIC-03-Vietnam-OSS-Final.pdf?sequence=2&isAllowed=y.

J. Youngman. 2016. A Good Tax: Legal and Policy Issues for the Property Tax in the United States. Cambridge: Lincoln Institute of Land Policy.

J.A. Zevenbergen. 2002. Systems of Land Registration. Aspects and Effects. Delft: NCG (Netherlands Geodetic Commission).